P9-CEQ-018

Keep

Paid

— Accent st —
Couching
Crewel Embroidery
Eyelet embroidery

Holbein Hans,
German painter and engraver
1497-1543 who was Court
Painter to Henry VIII from
1836 to 1543. He is noted
particularly for his portraits.

Renaissance Embroidery. A
form of cutwork in which
the design is outlined in
buttonhole st. before the ground
fabric is cut away. Parts of the
design are strengthened by
buttonhole bars.

*(Armenian edging   7th C St Ency/
and blanket st.   St p 110
(Antwerp st. ** p 111

Stranded floss
six-strand cotton thread for
embroidery. Threads can be
separated & used in twos or threes, etc.

star filling st.

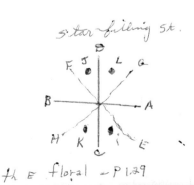

th E floral — P 129

The Stitchery Idea Book

The Stitchery Idea Book

Beverly Rush

VNR VAN NOSTRAND REINHOLD COMPANY

NEW YORK   CINCINNATI   TORONTO   LONDON   MELBOURNE

Motif by Mary Carol Mitchell. Motifs on pages
1 and 2 are by Mary Ann Spawn and Flo Wilson,
respectively.

Van Nostrand Reinhold Company Regional Offices:
New York Cincinnati Chicago Millbrae Dallas
Van Nostrand Reinhold Company International Offices:
London Toronto Melbourne

Copyright © 1974 by Litton Educational Publishing, Inc.
Library of Congress Catalog Card Number 74-1999
ISBN 0-442-27161-1

All rights reserved. No part of this work covered by the
copyright hereon may be reproduced or used in any form
or by any means—graphic, electronic, or mechanical,
including photocopying, recording, taping, or information
storage and retrieval systems—without written permission
of the publisher. Manufactured in the United States
of America

The authors and Van Nostrand Reinhold Company have
taken all possible care to trace the ownership of every
work of art included in this book and to make full
acknowledgment for its use. If any errors have accidentally
occurred they will be corrected in subsequent editions,
provided that notification is sent to the publisher.

Photographs by Beverly Rush, unless otherwise noted
Drawings by Jill Denny Nordfors
Designed by Jean Callan King/Visuality

Published by Van Nostrand Reinhold Company
A Division of Litton Education Publishing, Inc.
450 West 33rd Street, New York, N.Y. 10001
16 15 14 13 12 11 10 9 8 7 6 5 4 3 2

Library of Congress Cataloging in Publication Data

Rush, Beverly.
  The stitchery idea book.

  1. Needlework I. Title.
TT750.R87   746.4   74-1999
ISBN 0-442-27161-1

To all those who find pleasure and enrichment in creating beauty in their own way

ACKNOWLEDGMENTS

The greatest pleasure I have had while working on this book has been discovering the willingness of so many artists to share. To all those included, as well as those whose work there was not enough room for, I am deeply grateful.

To Jill Nordfors, Mary Ann Spawn, and Ann Spiess Mills I feel a special debt. I hope the rich joy of their art is apparent in the book.

To Patricia Rush, who typed from my jumbled notes and tapes until it made some sense; to Jean Wilson, Flo Wilson, Phalice Ayers, Janine Vincent, and Charlotte Machgan for their help and encouragement; to the Costume and Textile Study Collection at the University of Washington, and to Virginia Isham Harvey, its Preparator, and Diane Sugimura, go my appreciation.

My thanks go especially to Jacqueline Enthoven, who has given inspiration, ideas, sources, and love in abundance; to my family for their patience; and to my parents, who invested me with an immense sense of curiosity and interest in what can be created in this world.

Motif by Irene Ohashi.

Motif by Mrs. William L. Weed.

CONTENTS

FOREWORD

Many books have been written with emphasis on stitchery as a contemporary art form. Beverly Rush's *Stitchery Idea Book* has great appeal because it provides needed sources of inspiration for the decoration of clothes and the home. Folk-art embroidery brings joy and satisfaction into everyday life, enriching the lives of the originator as well as the beholder. We have all experienced the pleasure of admiring a beautiful purse or quilt made by a friend, and of seeing a young girl wearing a colorfully embroidered blouse or jeans.

For a while, the lifeless mechanical perfection of the industrial age gave disparaging connotations to "home-made" things, but the creative impulse dies hard. Today we are witnessing a joyful renaissance of folk art. Instead of condescending remarks on the "home-made" look, we now hear "did you really make it yourself?" with an admiring and somewhat envious tone of voice!

This book deserves to be widely used. The author's approach to design and color will prove to be particularly valuable. The photography is outstanding, the text filled with the joy of creating, and with inspiration for beginners as well as advanced stitchers.

Jacqueline Enthoven

Motif by Katherine Gorham.

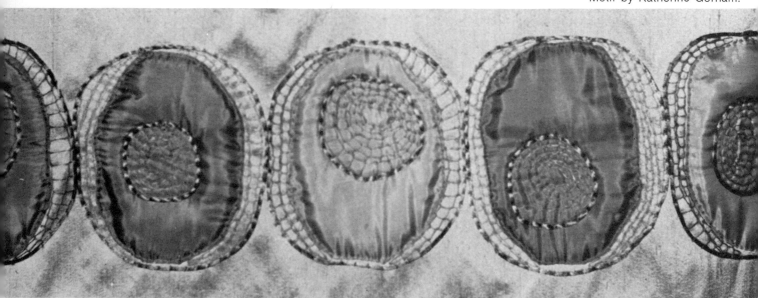

8

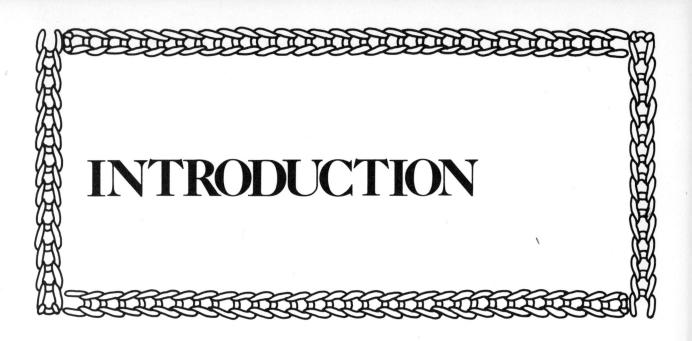

INTRODUCTION

This stitchery book is not meant to be used alone, but in conjunction with instruction books that explain the stitch techniques and how to construct the piece on which the embroidery is done. My whole conception was to provide something different from what bookstores and libraries are already full of—books that tell how to do techniques but are limited in showing ideas for using them. No book has space for everything, and if it leaves room for patterns and instructions for every example it must limit its examples, as well as duplicating all the rest of the craft books in its section on methods and techniques.

The aim of this book, then, is to present a collection of ideas with only general comments on each about materials and methods used to get particular effects. I hope that if you want to try your hand at one of these ideas, you will then search for a book or article on the specific method. So many craft instructions are now easily available that you should be able to find many technical details to help you explore your own ideas.

Embroidery has, of course, been used since earliest times to add beauty and decoration to clothing and articles in the home. Court ladies chatted together politely as they embroidered. Quilting bees were part of the social life of American Colonial days. For generations, stitches and samplers were an expected part of every young girl's education. Then, when machines outdid the evenest

of stitchers, anything made at home was suddenly out of vogue. Even the word *handmade* was no longer a compliment.

Now that machines are no longer a novelty, the value of things touched by the hand and mind of the craftsman is again appreciated. With wider travel and communication, more people are being exposed to cultures that have maintained their own folk art, rich with the lore and joy of a yesterday and today that is not so caught up in this modern, mass-production age. Such designs, made at home for personal use, tend to be spontaneous, with simple stitches and local materials.

Folk art, whether created in foreign lands or right in your own neighborhood, is a personal art formed of the symbols, traditions, and interests of the craftsman. The work in this book is really folk art in that sense, and I have used the word *artist* freely to describe the stitchers represented. Whether by professionals or beginners, the work shown here is far too diverse to have come from a single source, and each piece was chosen for the ideas it imparts. And, whether you are a stitcher from childhood, an artist in search of new media, or a total beginner, there is a wealth of material here to start you toward new ideas. Don't attempt to create a masterpiece or an heirloom. Just have fun. Your enjoyment of your art adds to the culture not only with what you create but with your new appreciation and financial support of what others are creating.

1 FOR THE HOME

Stitchery in the home can range from decorating a simple needle case to the artistic creation of large room dividers or fiber sculptures. But there seems to be a natural tendency to want to start with something small when trying a new idea, so let's begin with stitchery ideas for cards, books, gifts, and small home accessories. These might make good starting projects for children as well as adults, and the materials for small stitchery pieces are usually already on hand—scraps of felt, remnants of cloth, bits of ribbon and yarn. Once you have worked on things for your house, try some small stitchery gifts wrapped in stitchery.

Surface stitchery, canvaswork, and weaving are all manipulations of yarns or threads over a surface. Some of the motions may even be the same but called by different names in different crafts. Unless the background is completely covered, the choice of fabric to use for a stitchery becomes very important. Any of the textile techniques may be combined, such as adding stitchery to a needlepoint background, laying warp threads onto a fabric for needleweaving, or using a section of canvaswork as an appliqué. Look at every method with an open —and a roving—eye. Never let yourself be stopped by the rules. Stitchery can be worked on any materials that you can get a needle through, and with anything you can thread into a needle. If a fiber is too thick to pull through, it can be couched on. Stones, shells, glass, and other objects like beads can be attached to the background with various stitches.

Upholstery or drapery shops are rich sources of stitchery fabrics. For anything other than very large projects, watch for remnants or bolt ends. Discarded sample books can provide a whole collection for appliqué or patchwork. Handwoven or other nicely textured pieces might be found, and often in a beautiful range of colors. Rubberized backs on cloth present difficulty in getting the needle through, and should therefore be avoided. Loosely woven fabrics should be looked at with an eye toward drawn threadwork, which is either removing, pushing, or manipulating the woven threads in such a way that you can add woven, stitched, or appliqué areas. Sometimes a technical distinction is made between drawn threadwork, in which threads are removed, and drawn fabricwork, in which they are merely pushed from their woven places. If the threads are too firmly locked, the material cannot be used in either way. Open fabrics are also good sources for unraveling to use the threads for stitchery. Already color coordinated, the open weaves are more likely to use threads of interesting texture than tighter weaves.

There are so many mail-order outlets for yarn and stitchery supplies, that no stitcher is dependent on what can be found locally. Do not stop your search for materials at knitting yarns and embroidery floss. Become familiar with the various weights of Persian, crewel, and rya yarns. Thread of perle cotton comes in several weights and its twist makes it look new much longer than floss cotton. Visit weavers' shops; they will often sell you interesting yarns by the

Pin cushions, Mary Ann Spawn, 6 x 6 inches.
Materials: two pieces of velveteen, ribbons, stuffing.
Special Methods: decorations of ¾-inch, sequin-like paillettes, attached by the *shi-sha* method, which creates stitchery cups around them.

Greeting cards, Charlotte Machgan. *Materials:* fringed burlap, folded paper of card weight, to which the decorated burlap is glued. *Variation:* such cards are good for conveying stitchery messages to those with limited vision, who will appreciate the texture all the more.

One method of *shi-sha:* (left) hold the object or mirror to the fabric by laying two threads across the face. Then pass the thread across the surface twice more, at right angles to the first, whipping the thread over and back under, as shown. Enter each of the first holding threads into the fabric as nearly opposite its emergence as possible in order to create a secure cross tension to hold firmly (right). Then the Cretan stitch can be worked around the object, catching the fabric on one side and one of the crossed threads on the other.

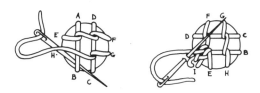

ounce, or thrums, which are yarn warp ends cut from the loom, and sold in combinations of colors and textures.

Yarn collecting might open some new doors on a trip or vacation, off the familiar tourist territory. You may discover not only some interesting yarns, but something more about the art done in an unfamiliar area, past or present. To share a common interest is a marvelous friendship bridge, even through a language barrier. Do a little investigating before going on your trip to find out what fibers, colors, and products are indigenous. Your interest

will be well rewarded with a useful set of yarn souvenirs. Since you cannot bring everything home, whether found nearby or far off, consider collecting a group of yarns that fit well together. Gather a complete scheme that combines a variety of shades, weights, and textures that could be used together. Write down any information needed to re-order if you need more. It is better to bring home five shades of one color, as they can always be used together, than to bring home five different colors, hoping to match or work them with other things.

Stitch for very long, and you will become a collector of fabrics and yarns. Collect for very long, and some need of organizing your things appears. A useful storage place for fabrics is a clear plastic garment bag with shelves instead of hangers. Being long and narrow, they take little space, but hold a surprising amount of fabrics, folded on the shelves, and easily visible for planning. Yarns might be divided into three groups: warm, cool, and neutral colors (see page 134). Kept in three hatboxes of clear plastic, the yarns can easily be seen for quick selection of a variety of shades. Large loops of yarn might be hung from racks or pegs meant for hats or cups.

Gift wrapping of stitchery, Anne Corbin. *Materials:* even-weave, mediumweight dress fabric with ready-made pom-pons added to the stitchery. The flap ends are held with a single contrasting cross-stitch. *Variations:* unwrapped, the decorative fabric can be made into a pillow or a small hanging—an additional gift.

Small box, by the author. *Materials:* unfinished box with recessed lid, Thai silk, silk and gold threads, colorful beads, padding, cardboard. *Special Methods:* after working the embroidery and padding and mounting it on cardboard cut to fit the recessed area, the section was held into place on stained box with double-faced carpet tape, removable when needed for occasional cleaning.

Needlecase, Eleanor A. Van de Water. Courtesy of DeLoris Stude. *Materials:* linen embroidered with yarn. *Special Methods:* the front and back covers are lined and left open at the inside fold, allowing cardboard to be inserted for book-like firmness, but removed for cleaning.

Scrapbook cover, Katherine Gorham. *Materials:* firm, lightweight cotton. *Special Methods:* material was batik-dyed first, then stitched decoratively to look like quilting. The cloth was mounted on the existing cover by the artist, and bound with decorative stitches of a firm cotton twist.

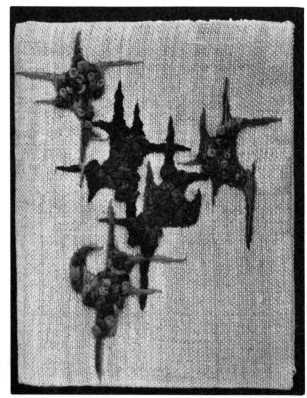

Book cover, Virginia B. Carter. *Materials:* raw silk, leatherwork of gold kid, Japanese and plate gold, rayon and silk threads, *shi-sha* mirrors. *Special Methods:* stitchery was padded and mounted on boards provided by a binder, and then book was bound in the bindery. Photo by James B. Carter.

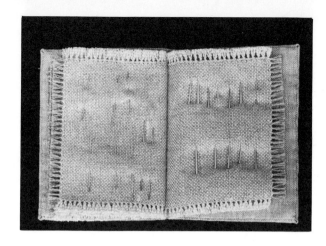

Needlecase open, showing the cloth pages holding needles.

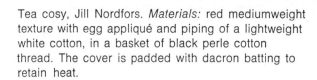
Tea cosy, Jill Nordfors. *Materials:* red mediumweight texture with egg appliqué and piping of a lightweight white cotton, in a basket of black perle cotton thread. The cover is padded with dacron batting to retain heat.

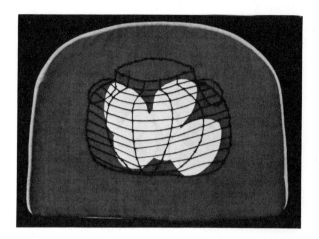

Hamper top, Jill Nordfors. *Materials:* mattress ticking, appliqué of lightweight cotton, stitchery in perle cotton. *Special Methods:* the entire top is padded with dacron batting and quilted for body. The sides are gathered onto an elastic band.

Appliquéd circles and strips form abstract tree shapes, Jill Nordfors. Courtesy of Barbara Meier. *Materials:* suede, wool knit, and lightweight cottons in raspberry tones on heavy khaki twill fabric. *Special Methods:* when the materials do not ravel badly, the edges do not have to be turned under and blind-stitched to the background. Instead a variety of decorative stitches can be used to cover the edges and attach the pieces to the background.

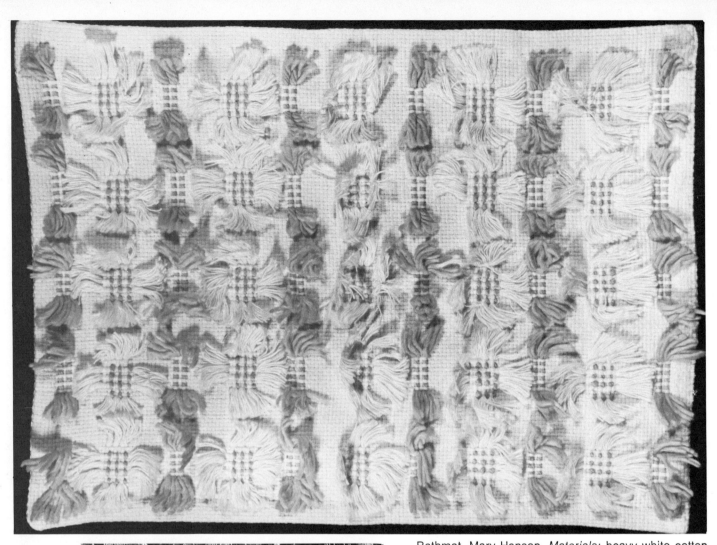

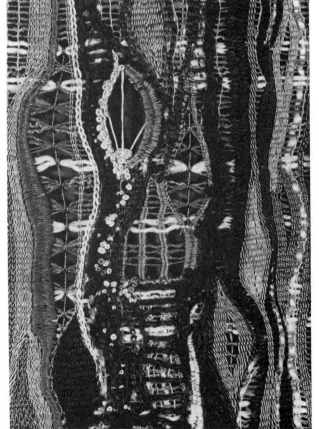

Bathmat, Mary Hanson. *Materials:* heavy white cotton yarn. *Special Methods:* the bathmat was handwoven, then a simple running stitch in contrasting thread was done in both horizontal and vertical directions, and cut so the ends of the thread make fringes. *Variation:* this can be spaced in various ways, over-all or as borders. Use only the vertical or horizontal stitches separately rather than crossing them, and vary the scale. Might be used on curtains, window or lamp shades, pillows or rugs.

Detail of drawn fabricwork by the author. Threads of a loosely woven fabric are pulled or manipulated to give an irregular surface for adding stitches to.

FURNISHINGS

Bedcovers, quilts, screens, room dividers, and upholstery can offer quite a challenge because of their large scale. Not only must the over-all stitchery design be planned more carefully, but material will have to be purchased in quantity before starting work. Consider whether your project can be broken down into smaller units—such as patch blocks for a patchwork quilt or pieces and panels for garments and accessories—embroidered, and then put together for the larger whole. Small units are easier to carry with you to work on while waiting for the dentist or the carpool, and psychologically, it is easier to tackle a series of small units than to be faced with an enormous area to be filled.

Stitchery of all sorts can be created for furnishings with simple techniques. Even a learner's sampler can result in a striking design for upholstery or screen panels, because it can be so easily adapted to the flat surfaces to be covered. You should pre-plan the method you want to use for mounting so that the proper allowance can be given at the edge of the background material for hems, seams, and other attachments.

New Mexican coverlet (*colcha*) made in 1740, collection of Mrs. Waldo Spiess. *Materials:* cotton, hand-dyed wools. *Special Methods:* according to Jacqueline Enthoven, the stitch used often on these *colchas* is the Bokhara stitch. It was so widely used in the coverlets, primarily because it reduces the amount of yarn (which was scarce) on the reverse side while covering the shape so completely, that it became known as the colcha stitch in New Mexico. The coverlet was made by a young bride from Spain, but the design of the sun (*sol*) motif shows Indian influence, suggesting that her slaves helped her.

Detail of the *colcha,* showing the background material and colcha stitch.

Bedspread, Carole Sabiston. *Materials:* Egyptian appliquéd panels were bought separately and applied to black velvet.

Patchwork

Patchwork is an old craft, which is currently undergoing great popularity. There are several ways to work patchwork, both on furnishings and clothing. The traditional method is to cut and seam the pieces together, either by hand or machine. The finished patchwork is frequently padded and backed, although this may not be necessary if the back will never be seen, as when the patchwork is being used for a seat cover. A second method involves marking the shape to be filled on muslin, pinning the pieces in the outline, and joining them with decorative embroidery or needle-lace stitches. The lightweight muslin forms an interfacing that holds the shape well for coats and vests. When the joinings are to be detached like needle lace, the beginning and ending yarns go through the muslin but are left unknotted. Once they are cut or pulled, the muslin falls away and the patches are held together by the joining stitches.

Pieced quilt, Dottie Harper. *Materials:* Sixty-three squares of different colored velvets, stitched in a variety of matching yarns, black velvet border. *Special Methods:* after stitching, the squares were joined, the border added, and the whole quilt backed and filled. *Variation* (shown): by attaching black velvet loops the quilt can be turned into a hanging.

Detail of 2-inch squares, each filled with a different stitch.

Seat cover stitched in a patchwork design, Phyllis Dodson. *Materials:* white linen divided with stitched squares, using over 150 different stitches, and finished with upholstery braid. *Special Methods:* mark the shape of the upholstery shape onto the linen, then block and mark the squares, approximately 2 x 2 inches. Fill each square with a different stitch or stitch combination, in various colors, but always with a border of red to form the grid pattern.

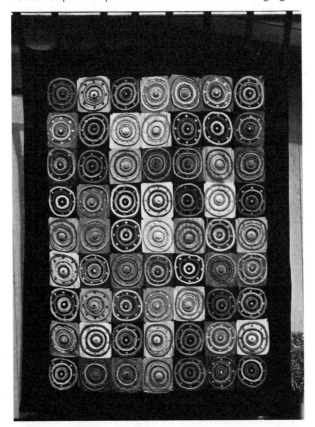

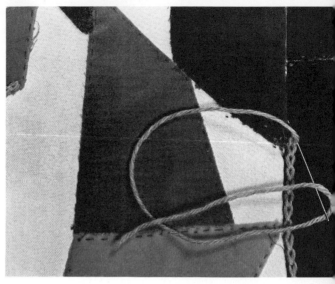

In a variation of traditional patchwork, in which the pieces are seamed directly to one another, velvet pieces are first basted to muslin, without turning under the edges, which are completely caught under the covering stitches. By Pat Albiston.

Then the cut edges are joined and embellished with decorative stitches.

Detail of pieced quilt showing decorative stitches used.

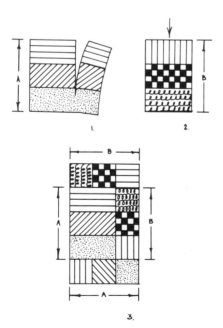

A method of working new designs in patchwork is to assemble pieces of roughly the same size, then cut and rearrange to form interesting new patterns.

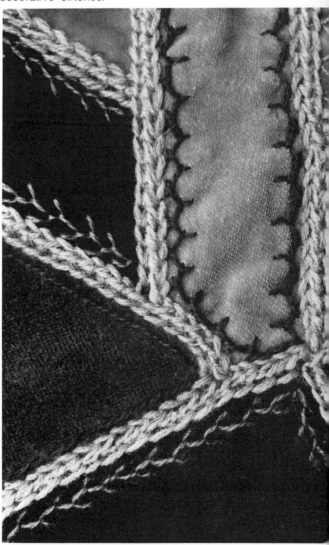

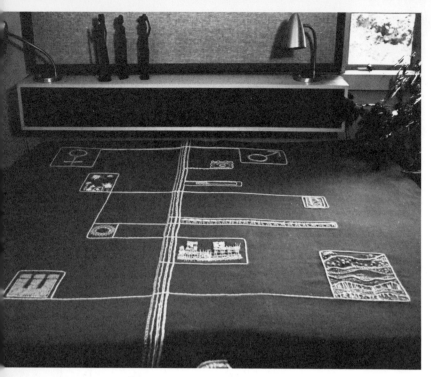

Contemporary-styled bedspread, Jean Wilson.
Materials: two pieces of rust-colored fleece coat
fabric, joined together with a decorative stitch. More
stitchery is added for design.

Traditional New England styled bedspread, Phalice
Ayers, designed by Catherine Hedlund. *Materials:*
pale green wool twill, white thread in native-flower
designs.

Designs and Materials

In furnishings, design may come from any source.
With modern transportation, stitchery work done or
found in other countries and other ages often appears in our shops, perhaps meant for a purpose
we no longer have or understand, and can be incorporated into a contemporary work with very
decorative results.

In creating a design for furnishings, relate it to
the room where the piece will be, the lighting it will
be seen under, and the style of furniture it may be
mounted on. Where wood of the supporting piece
may show, as in screens or chairs, both the background material and the boldness or delicacy of the
stitchery should suit the wood design. The structure
and carving may be formal or contemporary, simple
or elaborate.

In working the design for a screen or hanging
with large unbroken areas, or one where the fabric
covers all the existing structure, the stitchery motif
might be simplified and worked on a fairly bold
scale, or single units of design might be scattered
attractively across the surface. When the background fabric of the stitchery is especially interesting, a top border of stitches might be all that is
necessary to create a striking effect, as for example, on screens made to have no exposed wood
except legs, if they have them. They are entirely
"upholstered," and the fabric selection naturally
would be a major consideration in choosing your
design.

Materials can vary widely, but if the stitchery is
to get heavy wear, like a seat cushion, durability
must be a basic consideration. A chair in a little-
used visiting room can be worked in more delicate
materials than a footstool in the family's playroom.
In all stitchery, the amount of wearability depends
on the quality and amount of wool or other yarn on
the surface. A tightly worked piece made with firm
yarn that is thick enough to fill the spaces well will
still be lovely after many years' use.

The quality and firmness of all exposed surfaces
are important, whether these are the background or
the stitches, and whether the piece is in canvaswork or embroidery. A firm yarn with a good even
twist, even if it is a fine yarn, will wear better than one
of loose strands and soft surfaces. The stitches
should be worked with ample yarn on the surface
and be firmly anchored. Stitches with long detached
threads should be avoided because the detached
part can catch and pull. Consider comfort, too.
French knots and stitchery with a highly uneven
texture are not pleasant to sit on.

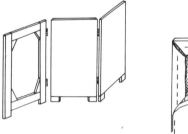
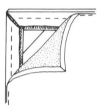

Making an upholstered screen: (left) inside construction detail of screen, (right) linen from the front of the screen has been pulled over bars and stapled to the back. The back lining can then be stapled or tacked to the edges.

Oriental-styled screen, Marjorie Weed. *Materials:* linen, crewel wool, mostly in the long and short stitch, constructed 3-paneled screen frame. *Special Methods:* build a simple framework of wood, as shown in the drawing, with enough bracing to be sturdy. Cut the front fabric the size of the screen section, plus allowance for stretching around the frame, and tacking or stapling 2 inches to the back of the wood. Cut the back fabric, which may be different from the front fabric, the same size as the screen section with allowance enough for turning under efficiently. Then draw your design on paper, trace it with dressmaker's carbon across the 3 front panels, and after the design has been worked, stretch each front section onto the frame. First staple the center sides and center top and bottom, then continue pulling taut along the straight of the fabric, stapling as you go, and finally miter the corners. Tuck the back fabric, with mitered corners, smoothly into place along the edge, and fasten with small tacks or staples (later covered with braid) or decorative upholsterer's nails. *Variations:* this same method of stretching, mitering, and tacking into place can be used in covering many small chair seats. Some seats merely lift out of their wooden frame, and others must be unscrewed from underneath.

Framed screen, June McLean (June of California), 3½ x 5 feet. *Materials:* linen, wool, silk, and acrylic yarns using 19 shades of green providing good contrast, worked in straight and Cretan stitches and Turkey-work. *Special Methods:* the screen was worked in 3 panels, but framed as a single unit, and is meant to be hung. Photo by Barbara Brogliati.

Canvaswork and Appliqué

Needlepoint or canvaswork is in much prominence today, and has possibilities not often tried. The canvas itself may be double or single weave, and made of cotton, linen, hemp, flax, silk, or gauze. Most of what we see today is cotton, and the size is measured by the numbers of holes to the inch. A wide number of stitches can be used; the general criterion for choosing is whether the stitch hides the canvas. Needlepoint usually refers to work all of tent stitch, whether gros point or petit point. Canvaswork, or canvas embroidery, is broader, implying any work done using canvas as a base, and includes needlepoint, crewelwork, and bargello. Canvaswork can be used by itself, or in smaller pieces as appliqués.

Appliqué is a good solution where outdoor or nursery furnishings need a firm, tough fabric, such as vinyl or tent and awning canvas, that is difficult for stitchery because of its weave or texture. But a bold appliqué design in bright, contrasting colors can be machine stitched in place, and will take much abuse without showing the effects. The appliqué can also consist of a piece of stitchery or needlepoint done on a panel that can be blind-stitched to the upholstery fabric in the center of the back, seat, or arms of a chair. This would at least protect the stitchery from the rough wear that edges of furniture get.

Appliqué is the method of attaching a separate piece of fabric, leather, or other flexible material to the ground cloth. Appliqué is more efficient than stitchery for filling large areas, because the whole area can be filled at once with a single large piece or several pieces rather than having to work it back and forth with thread or yarn. The result is lighter than it would be with stitchery. The ornately embroidered garments one sees in old protraits of royalty were very heavy and warm to wear. But even in appliqué, the weight of the ground fabric should be sturdy enough to hold the applied fabrics without sagging.

Appliqué can be applied with a blind-stitch or running-stitch, usually on turned-under edges. Cottons tend to be easiest to work with, as is cotton thread. Turning under is necesary with materials that ravel. Silks, synthetics, and loose weaves are the worst. Blind-stitch has a slightly puffy look, and running-stitch has characteristic dimples at each stitch. Appliqués can be overstitched decoratively without turning under the edges when the material will not ravel easily, as with felt, suede, velvet, knits, and some cottons, or they can be bonded on with fabric adhesive. If attaching by machine, several stitches can be used. Just plain straight stitches can be run around and around over the edges, forming a network of slightly irregular lines hiding

Contemporary bench by Judith Berni Anderson. *Materials:* penelope canvas, filled with rows of sampler stitches, and mounted on a custom-made low bench. *Variations:* benches of many sizes and proportions offer a flat, uncluttered surface, which provides a good base for a strong design.

Child's room seat cover, Jean Kendall. *Materials:* wool on canvas, worked in tent stitch with decorative stitches added to increase patchwork effect. *Special Methods:* design for canvaswork was taken from the child's painting shown at upper left.

the edge. The satin-stitch is commonly used, as are other decorative stitches or combinations of stitches. If one row is not sufficient, use several, perhaps even several colors of thread. Using the wide zigzag, or a long straight stitch, it would also be possible to thread or whip heavier yarns through by hand. By removing the presser foot, you can use the machine in a free embroidery style over the edges, forming curly, loopy lines, wavy squiggles, or lightening jags going back and forth at perpendicular

Needlepoint seat cover and back panel for antique chair, Jean Kendall. *Materials:* wool on canvas, worked in tent-stitch. *Special Methods:* chair design was adapted from Oriental rug shown.

Cushion and arm panels for French cane-backed chair, Phyllis Dodson. *Materials:* antique satin, crewel wool.

Upholstery for wing-backed chair, Phalice Ayers. *Materials:* blue linen with crewel yarns of a range of values from blue to white. Typical of New England design, with a great deal of New England laid stitch.

Upholstery for small-scaled chair, Phalice Ayers, designed by Catherine Hedlund. *Materials:* linen, crewel yarn. *Special Methods:* the design for the ¾-sized chair, a copy of one of the small chairs New England peddlers carried to show their wares, is appropriately taken from the Thornton Burgess children's stories.

angles to the edge. All of these can be embellished with various hand stitches or knots. Jean Ray Laury's book *Appliqué Stitchery* is one that can fill you in on the details of appliqué technique.

In using appliqué for design, the main interest should come from the cut shapes, which can achieve free, contemporary looks with clean splashes of color, or formal looks with even, smaller pieces. The stitches should be for texture and surface enrichment only. Simple designs work best, as the technique lends itself to clean-cut bold shapes. Cut large design pieces with the grain of the fabric going the same way as on the ground for best results in keeping the appliqué flat. Appliqués are not necessarily flat, since padded and quilted shapes can also be used. In addition to regular appliqué there is reverse appliqué, in which you start with layers of all the fabrics you will be using, usually three to five. Then you cut away design shapes to whatever layer has the color you want in that area. Appliqué and reverse appliqué can be combined, building up some areas, cutting into others.

Upholstery for traditional chair, Phalice Ayers. *Materials:* green wool background, stitched with blue silk thread. *Special Methods:* the form of quilting called trapunto is done by outlining the design in running stitch through at least two layers of cloth, and padding it from the underside. *Variation:* trapunto is also effective worked on a printed fabric for upholstery.

Trapunto and Italian Quilting
Trapunto is a stitchery technique that can be very well adapted to upholstery. You will need three layers for trapunto: the surface fabric, a padding layer, such as dacron batting, and a backing or lining layer. Sandwiching all three layers together, stitch through all three by hand or machine, completely outlining the design. Then, taking care not to clip either fabric, cut all the padding away from the outside of the design stitching, as close to the stitching as possible. A second method is to sew the two layers together, surface and lining, along the design lines. The back is then slit wherever necessary and the padding inserted. The slits are closed by whipping together, and some tacking may be added to hold the padding in place. The lining material should be chosen so as not to ravel or fray easily, so that the hand stitching will hold.

Narrow, parallel lines, perhaps ⅛-inch apart, can be sewn through the two layers of fabric with yarns or cord threaded to make raised-line designs, called Italian quilting, a technique related to trapunto. The lines could run straight, curve, or zig-zag. If this method is used with a sheer fabric on top, such as organdy, and colored yarns pulled through, a pleasant result will be achieved.

MOUNTING PANELS
Using a crosspiece in a hem is one of the commonest methods of mounting hangings, and can also be applied to panels or banners for screens and room dividers. For a hanging, a dowel or a curtain rod is slipped inside a top hem that has been left open at the edges. The cord to be used as a hanger can be wrapped around each end of the dowel, and slipped over a nail, like a picture-frame hanger. Decorative screens are sometimes planned to include a fabric panel as part of the design. These screens vary from smaller shutter units for windows to full length oversized antique screens built for large rooms and tall ceilings. On some, the fabric insert is only a portion with most of the screen being wood, often carved and quite decorative. On others, the wood framing is only on the edges as a support for a full fabric screen. Doors on bookcases and hutches from past years also may have been built to incorporate decorative fabrics. To mount a panel on these screens, make a top and bottom hem for rods to hold the piece in place. If the fabric is wider than the rod it will push together when mounted, producing a gathered effect. Interesting results can be achieved with several appliquéd layers of semi-sheer material, built up also with surface work, which allow light to filter through. A heavy upholstery-weave fabric or canvaswork would be more appropriate to an ungathered panel or banner.

Room dividers are related to screens in that both are used to break up space in a room area, but differ in that they are not freestanding. A room divider is usually suspended from a crosspiece, like a hanging. It may be held straight by weights or a second rod across the bottom, or it may hang freely, which allows it to move slightly with any breeze. If it is hung as separate parts or as one piece with large slits, people can walk through it. The creation of these hangings is very different from other panels we have described because they are worked to be seen from both sides. The design and the mounting must be carried out with this in mind.

Hanging panel, St. Francis and the animals, Ann Spiess Mills. *Materials:* various yarns on felt. *Special Methods:* the simplest way to hang a panel is from rings.

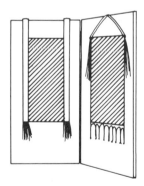

Simple ways of hanging a panel on a screen: (left) by embroidered edgings or tapes continued up to the top of the screen, (right) by two cords, one at each end of a dowel inserted in a hem.

Hanging of drawn threadwork, meant to be seen from both sides, Fritzi Oxley. *Special Methods:* hanging is suspended from a glass rod instead of a dowel. The rod is inserted in a plastic standard, a free-standing structure that can be moved about easily for the best placement.

If you don't want to start from scratch, but would like to mount a smaller area of stitchery on an already standing screen, there are a number of ways to do it. Appliqué techniques, such as those you might use to put a panel on a piece of furniture, would be appropriate for incorporating finished embroidery panels on the face of a screen. Instead of appliqué, a banner may be hung on one section of a screen. The other sections could be left plain, or a series could be grouped on the different panels, perhaps with a unifying theme such as the seasons of the year. If such a panel is full length, then the top of the fabric can be tacked or stapled along the top piece of the screen, while the bottom hangs free, elaborated with tassels, knotting, or fringes. Wherever there is a solid area, small nails or tacks can be used to mount the piece, as long as they don't show. Knotting and other edgings can sometimes be tied to various surfaces of the screen, thus contributing to the mounting.

Hanging of velvet patchwork, Jill Nordfors. *Special Methods:* the hanging has self loops hung on a stained dowel. Dowels are inexpensive, widely available in an assortment of sizes, and can be hung on the wall, or hung from the top with cords.

Antique screen to cover fireplace in summer, Jo Reimer. *Materials:* background of cotton, appliquéd layers of sheer materials. *Special Methods:* the panels are partly machine-stitched, and are hung on dowels through both top and bottom hems.

Detail of stitching in the screen, showing how the poppy shapes are created by couching down heavy threads.

Room divider, Carole Sabiston, 7 x 9 feet. *Materials:* firmly woven, textured cotton, hanks of goat's lamb's, and sheep's wool. *Special Methods:* the hanging, meant to be seen from both sides, was cut out of two pieces of matching material, stitched along the sides but left open at the ends, turned, and top-stitched ½-inch from each edge. The center holes were cut out and strengthened with narrow slats of wood, as shown in the diagram, and then the edges were zig-zig stitched closed. Top and bottom hem sections are held in place by slats of wood extending the full width, also used for hanging and weighting the bottom. Randomly knotted and twisted wool was couched down on the front, and left hanging freely, wrapped in places, on the back (not shown).

Wood slats inserted in the room divider sections to hold shape.

Detail of figure and border in panel, showing design adapted from antique Oriental panel. Figure is in stem-stitch, and border consists of two parallel rows of running stitches, threaded first with heavy yarn and then with very fine gold thread (see diagram).

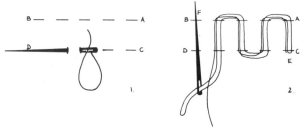

Free-hanging screen panel, Judith Berni Anderson. *Materials:* linen, wool yarn, and gold thread. *Special Methods:* since this panel hangs against the louvered screen, it is simply tacked into a wooden piece and hung on a ring; lower edge is fringed.

Threaded running stitch, as used for border in the screen panel: (1) double row of running stitch in lightweight thread for the foundation, (2) threading back and forth, through parallel rows, first with a heavy yarn, then following in the same steps with a fine gold thread. *Variations:* many stitches or stitch variations might be formed into a border.

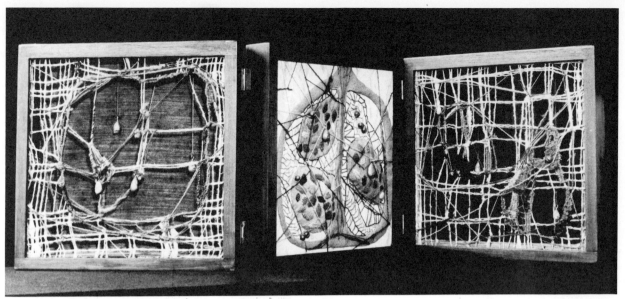

Altar triptych, Jorjanna Lundgren, 13 x 39 inches.
Materials: constructed wood frame with hinges,
loose-weave drapery fabric, appliqués of various
fabrics, wool yarn, fishing weights. *Special Methods:*
center section, depicting a pomegranate, which
is an ancient symbol of the Resurrection, has
stitchery, appliqués, and fishing weights rubbed with
gold as seeds. The end panels of this Easter triptych
employ various forms of needleweaving, and were
tacked inside of the deep frame, giving a shadow-box
effect. Photo by Richard E. Kephart.

Wonderful World of Warren and Wesley, Helen J.
Rumpel. *Special Methods:* design was inspired by
drawings the artist's sons had done during their
first years in school. Each panel was worked and
mounted individually, then the whole encompassed
in an irregular shape.

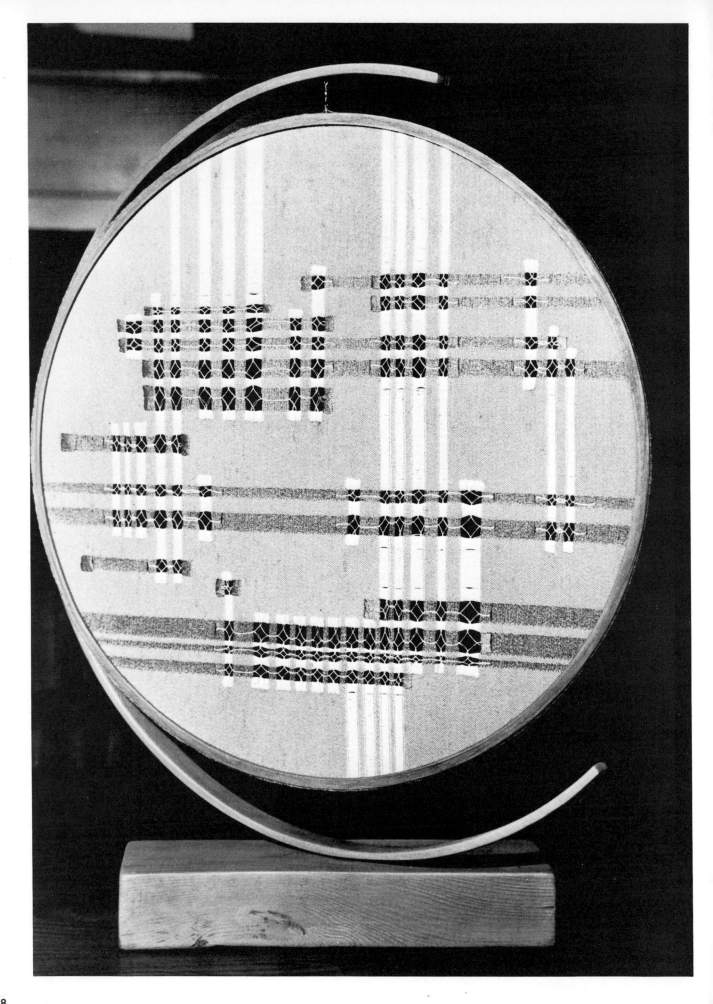

Silent Gong, drawn threadwork, Fritzi Oxley. *Materials:* antique satin, which is gold on one side, white on the other. *Special Methods:* hanging is mounted in an embroidery hoop, and suspended from a section of a larger embroidery hoop, with a fishing swivel that allows the design to reverse its field as it swings gently back to front. *Variation:* a very large-scaled circle might be hung from a high ceiling in the same manner, to reverse slowly with the air currents.

Two details, one from each side of the drawn threadwork.

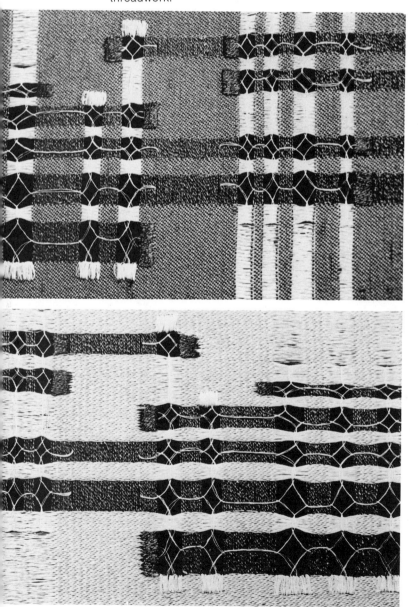

Tom Tom Top, Fritzi Oxley. *Materials:* white stitches on white wool, embroidery hoop, fringing and suspension cord of same yarn.

Needlewoven hanging, Jo Reimer. *Special Methods:* both embroidery hoops are used for mounting. Fabric is mounted across the back of the hoop and is seen through the needleweaving. The outside ring is trimmed with a velvet ribbon. Decorative hook is used for hanging.

Detail of finished edge of hoop.

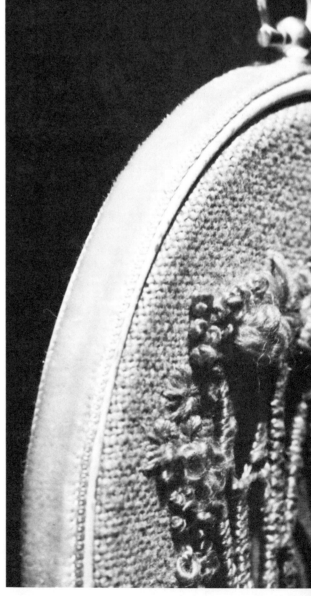

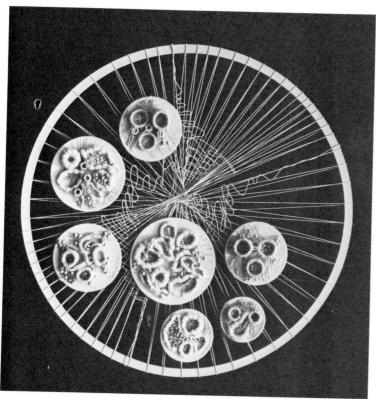

Needlewoven hoop, Jo Reimer. *Materials:* 3-foot
hoop strung with cotton cord. Islands are embroidery
hoops covered after working the fabric, and attached
to the strung cords. The airy needleweaving adds
balance. *Special Methods:* warp has been strung
across the hoop, then covered islands of related
shapes and free-form needleweaving were added.

Universe and Sun, Helen J. Rumpel. *Materials:*
Finnish linen, two sizes of embroidery hoops,
finished front and back.

SHAPED STITCHERY FOR DECORATIONS

Stitchery does not have to be done on a flat background. Anything that can be made or shaped of cloth can have stitchery added for decoration or definition. The construction of the piece is usually planned in advance so that most of stitching can be done while the part being decorated can still be held flat. For example, the simplest shaped stitchery would be an ornament made from two pieces of felt cut together in a circle or other simple shape, embroidered separately, stitched together, and stuffed. You might have the design on the front

Baseball Christmas decoration, Marie L. Filip.
Materials: Polyester-fiber stuffed ball, about size of regulation hardball, felt pieces cut in pentagons.
Special Methods: each section, with a different motif, is joined to others with the antique seam stitch.

Heart-shaped Christmas ornaments, Ann Spiess Mills.
Materials: felt, various yarns for decorating front piece and making stitchery border.

only, or on both front and back. The decision depends on how the object is to be used, and how much time you wish to invest in it. After the design has been worked, sew the two pieces together, leaving enough opening to insert cotton or dacron for stuffing. Since felt doesn't ravel, it can be sewn with an outside seam, perhaps with a buttonhole-stitch or some other decorative stitch. If you are using fabric that can ravel, place the two pieces of decorated material with outside surfaces together, stitch a seam around three sides, turn, stuff, and stitch the fourth side closed with a blind-stitch.

Now, what can you do with this shape? If you made it very big, it's a pillow, if you made it very small, it's an ornament to be hung on a Christmas tree or a Valentine's day display, or over a baby's crib. There is a natural tendency to feel most free and to have the most fun doing something temporary and festive for a holiday, so why not start with a decoration to be hung or used as part of a festive arrangement? Small stitchery ornaments make excellent gifts, any time of the year, and can be personalized with figures or motifs when given for a birthday or anniversary.

Textile objects of all sorts can be enriched with stitchery, from the simplest of children's dolls or animal toys to the character dolls collected by adults. The animal and plant worlds are full of friendly living creatures that can serve as models for dolls or even abstract forms. Design possibilities are almost unlimited in the contemporary and ingenious soft sculptures that stand free in the middle of a room, or when used as three-dimensional hangings, swing from the ceiling, in the fashion the traditional Mexican piñatas.

Ornaments, Irene Ohashi. *Materials:* felt, perle cotton, and wool yarns for working decorations front and back.

Sampler pillow, Charlotte Machgan. *Materials:* burlap with wool yarns.

Pictures on the following pages:

1
Quilt, Mary Ann Spawn. Photograph by Douglas Spawn. The quilt is made of embellished decorator's swatches of antique satin and is bordered in fake fur.

2
Carved corner chair with stitchery seat by Katherine Gorham.

3
Fireplace screen for summer use, Jo Reimer. An antique screen was rehung with stitched and appliquéd layers of semi-sheer fabric.

4
Quilt, Irene Ohashi. A series of 48 pillows were whip-stitched together by hand, and clusters of French knots or tassels added to corners.

5
Joy, small fiber sculpture, Fritzi Oxley. An acrylic photo-display cube was covered with canvas embroidery, and purchased flowers for dress trim were re-embroidered to match and added.

6
Tray cover and tea cosy from India, courtesy of the Costume and Textile Study Collection, School of Home Economics, University of Washington.

7
Vest by Diane Katz. Navy suede is lined with taffeta, and braided ties are made of yarn used for stitchery.

8
Crazy-quilt patchwork vest, Linda Batway. Not true patchwork, this was made by basting patches to muslin that had been cut in pattern of vest.

9
Vest woven from the center out to a planned shape, by Barbara Meier.

10
Appliquéd overblouse, Jill Nordfors.

1

2

3

4

5

6

7

8

9

10

One-piece dolls, cut free-hand, sewn, and stitched by Susan and Karen Thompson, aged 11 and 12. *Materials:* cotton, muslin, embroidery thread. *Special Methods:* cut two pieces of material in the desired shape, stitch for decoration. Place two pieces with right sides together, sew, turn, stuff, and finish off by blind-stitching. *Variation:* if the dolls are to be washable, so should all threads, materials, and stuffing.

Simple dolls, Irene Ohashi. *Materials:* Even-weave dress fabric, trimmed with cut felt shapes and stitches of various yarns. *Special Methods:* made on the same principles as the children's dolls, these have a circular piece of cardboard sewn in at the base to give the doll a way to stand. *Variation:* washable dolls can have bases of firm plastic instead of cardboard.

Santera figure, Helen J. Rumpel, 2 feet high.
Materials: cotton with stitched and appliquéd design,
stuffed with dacron. *Special Methods:* contemporary
design of doll is based on the New Mexico custom
of making doll images of female saints.

Nativity grouping, based on figures in Mexican-Spanish folklore, Ann Spiess Mills, 4 inches at highest point, courtesy of Mrs. Jack Taylor Dempsey. *Materials:* felt, wool yarn, oil pastels to tint faces, cotton stuffing.

Shepherd and shepherdess with their sheep, from same grouping, Ann Spiess Mills.

Tiny Christ child, tucked in basket, Ann Spiess Mills.

Angel with mandolin, Ann Spiess Mills, approximately
19 inches tall, courtesy of Mrs. Benny Ross.
Materials: outer fabric and lining of felt, embroidery
thread, stuffing. *Special Methods:* the body shape,
including the head, dress, and sleeves are cut
in a single piece, one for the front and one for the
back. The skirt is left open at the bottom, to allow
the angel to be used on a tree-top for Christmas.
Separate arms are made, stuffed and inserted into the
sleeve. A separate panel is put on the skirt front
for a color change. The wings and halo (shown in
back view) as well as the mandolin are made
separately and attached to the body. The pieces are
joined with buttonhole-stitches; the angel's curls
are all French knots.

Back view of the angel, showing construction of
wings, halo, and Mrs. Mill's symbolic decorations,
which often include thistles, one of the flowers of
Mary, ladybugs, representing the beast of the Lord,
and the bluebird of happiness.

Santa Claus, Mary Ann Spawn. *Materials:* red velvet, nylon stocking face, "leather" boots and belt. *Special Methods:* mounted on a rod, the figure moves up and down in his wood chimney base. Gloves, coat front, pants legs, and black velvet bag of toys are all embroidered. Miniature packages and a tiny rocking horse spill out of the bag, adding to the spirit of the piece.

Old-fashioned dolls, JoAnne S. Haldeman. *Materials:* muslin body and faces, cotton prints and patchwork for clothing.

Flora, Janet Wetzig Collins. *Materials:* felt face and body, various yarns and materials. *Special Methods:* to create the character of a middle-aged Spanish dancer, each hair was sewn in one thread at a time, allowing a mixture of black and gray, and eyelashes were made of cut Turkey-work in a heavy-duty polyester sewing thread. After the face was worked, the body/head was stuffed, then arms and legs put on. The doll was dressed last, in a skirt with a large embroidered rose at the back.

Orange Herbert, Mary Ann Spawn. *Materials:* textured and plain upholstery velvet in the same color, various yarns and shredded nylon stockings for stuffing. *Special Methods:* the body and head are cut in one unit. The two egg shaped, oval pieces—one for the front and one for the back—are cut flat at the bottom curve to allow for sitting. The smoother velvet is appliquéd on the top section and heavily stitched, for the face. Arms, hands, legs, feet, and banana are all sewn and stuffed separately, then joined to the stuffed body/head shape. Both machine and hand sewing were used. Joinings were covered with fur-like, cut-pile stitches.

Friendly Bird, movable children's toy, Mary Ann Spawn. *Materials:* upholstery velvet, yarn, felt, knitting needle, hollow cone, wound once with string. *Special Methods:* bird is made so that the expandable velvet neck can bob up and down from nest of yarn. Bird is mounted on a long knitting needle that extends from the bottom of the cone, and can be manipulated by hand, to the delight of children.

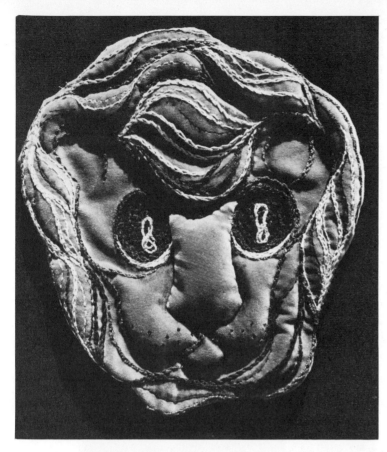

Lion's head, Carol Weyhrich. *Materials:* velveteen, padding. *Special Methods:* quilting done with decorative stitches adding dimension and contours to the lion's face.

Hoss, Helen J. Rumpel. *Materials:* yarn, woven wool tweed, fake fur blanket, tail in a snood of detached buttonhole-stitch.

Shaped ornaments, Pat Albiston. *Materials:* 3-inch rings, beads, yarn, gold thread. *Special Methods:* the rings are covered by wrapping or buttonholing, then threads are laid across for needleweaving the center space. *Variations:* any ring can be used, including dime-store bangle bracelets and wood curtain rings. Shapes can be used as window pulls or even as jewelry.

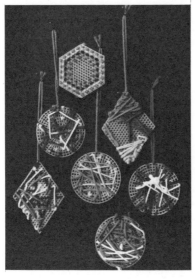

Shaped flower ornament, Anne Corbin. *Materials:* variety of fabrics, wool and cotton, plain and figured. *Special Methods:* created by an exaggerated trapunto method, the front patchwork of pieces was laid over the solid but shaped back, and the front pieces stitched to one another through both layers. Then the back of each area was split, stuffed, and resewn, making the piece quite highly padded. *Variations:* the back lining can be plain if it is to be displayed against a wall, or the front fabrics repeated and the slits decorated with stitches to be hung free in space.

Shaped ornaments, nursery school children. *Materials:* plastic grids, such as those found in craft shops, yarns. *Variations:* the evenness of the grid might lend itself well to canvas stitches.

New Mexican tin cross, about 1920, refilled by Ann Spiess Mills. *Materials:* originally filled with decorated paper; refilled with stitchery on blue velvet.

Framed padded hanging, Fritzi Oxley. *Materials:* silk cameo has "hair" of raw silk, and is against a "wallpaper" striped pattern of embroidery thread on silk; the oval is recessed in brown silk and framed.

Chessboard in needlepoint, Judith Berni Anderson.
Materials: custom-made box with recessed center
area, canvas and wool yarns, glue.

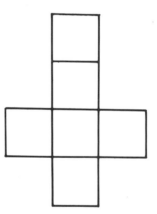

Shape to be worked for covering a cube. Measure
your own cube, making each square section the
same size. Cut, adding a small seam allowance where
pieces are to be joined, and fit to the cube as shown.

Mouse in House, shaped stitchery, Judith Weston.
Materials: covered acrylic photo-display cube, stuffed
toy mouse, wool, horsehair, twigs, moss, hay, dried
corn kernels. *Special Methods:* the cube was
covered with brown wool (see diagram), a variety of
chunky stitches were made in heavy wools, including
the couching on of small accent twigs and moss,
and a nest was made (inside the cube) of horsehair,
hay, and even a few grains of corn for the mouse.
Courtesy Lauralee R. Murphy.

Portrait of an Agnostic, shaped stitchery, Jorjanna
Lundgren. *Materials:* woolen and velvet fabrics,
rayon and linen threads, sand-filled boxes for
shaping, three *milagros,* which are small silver pieces,
used by some Mexicans as symbolic prayers to
leave in churches. *Special Methods:* each side of the
separate cubes was worked individually, then sewn
together to fit over the weighted boxes. The surface
decoration was created to integrate the multiple
units, without losing their individuality. The silver eyes,
arm and leg were incorporated with the stitchery.
Photo by Richard E. Kephart.

2 STITCHERY ON CLOTHING

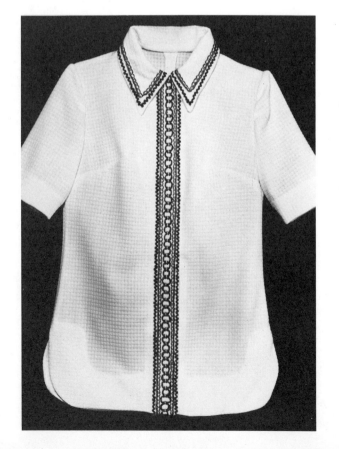

The earliest use of embroidery was undoubtedly for decorating clothing. Before printing was developed, the only way to add design to cloth was by weaving it in, by painting, or by embroidery. In an age of mass production, stitchery can add an individual or personalized touch to home-made garments, even to purchased ready-made clothing, by embellishing, strengthening design lines, or shifting attention away from a line that seems unflattering or too harsh. It can modify color effects or add new colors. If bright colors seem stark where they join, they can be blended with an interchange of these colors, across the joining line or seam. In ready-made clothes, instead of ending a part of the design at the seam line, carry the shape across with stitchery. Add a new embroidered fabric inset in a skirt or a length to a hem. You might even like such a worked-over dress better than its original.

Handmade polyester double-knit shirt, border by Jean Kelso. *Materials:* boilfast cotton floss in three simple stitches but a full spectrum of colors.

Handmade dress, Carole Sabiston. *Materials:* tussah silk from India, perle cotton thread. *Special Methods:* the mosaic-like clusters of stitches, in tones analogous to the dress, ease the transition across the color change.

Back view of the dress.

Handwoven skirt with stitchery texturing by Helen J. Rumpel. *Materials:* even-weave striped fabric, yarn. *Special Methods:* eighteen different stitches were worked, one on each yellow stripe of the cloth.

Handmade jumper, Mary Carol Mitchell. *Materials:* wool jumper with dark green stitchery panel. The panel is sewn into the waist seam, and finished with a tiny suede tie belt. *Variation:* it would be possible to suspend the panel from a belt, allowing it to be detached and hung on the wall when not being worn. Belt ends would fold behind panel.

Handmade linen dress, inset piece embroidered by the author. *Materials:* green linen, white perle cotton. *Special Methods:* the design was contrived by arranging various sizes of paper circles and marking with dressmaker's carbon. The circles were worked in a variety of stitches, then the wavy lines filled in The embroidery was completed before cutting and sewing into dress.

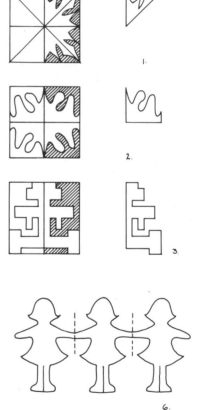

Handmade dress, Virginia Thorne. *Special Methods:* the design was arrived at by folding and cutting paper, just as children make paper dolls or snowflakes (see diagram). Such designs may be transferred by basting along the outer edge of the cut paper, which is pinned into place. Any design drawn on a paper pattern may be transferred with dressmaker's carbon. A ballpoint pen (best if an empty pen) makes a good tool for this, rather than the commonly used tracing wheel. There are also new pencils, whose marks transfer when the heat of an iron is applied, available in some embroidery outlets. *Variations:* cut-and-folded patterns are used in Hawaii for making quilts, but the designs are used as appliqué, or several layers applied to make reverse appliqué by cutting away shapes.

Cut-paper shapes that can be arranged for stitchery designs: (1) paper folded in eighths and cut—also try starting with a circle. (2) folded in fourths and cut, (3) folded in half and cut, (4) positive shape dissected, rearranged, and used with negative shape, (5) separate, related shapes cut and arranged, (6, 7) accordian-folded paper cut to a single shape to form repeated motif.

DESIGN SOURCES
Designs come from many sources. Jewelry from ancient times and other cultures can be a rich source of design ideas for adapting to stitchery. Clothes from other countries, either ancient or modern costumes, can inspire new ideas. The purpose in using these designs is not to recreate the costume but to simplify or find a single unit of decoration that can be adapted to contemporary use.

Appliquéd cattle trapping (ornamental cloth) from India, courtesy of the Costume and Textile Study Collection, School of Home Economics, University of Washington. Notice the outer square of small stylized elephants, done in different colors, and the easy-to-make but very effective border of triangles (see drawing).

Drawing for a border in appliqué. The strip is clipped at even intervals along one edge. The depth of the clipping should equal one-half of the distance from one clip to the next. The corners of each section are folded toward each other until they meet. For a very flat edge, the strip can be cut, folded, pressed into place, and applied with a blind-stitch. Or the strip may be clipped, pinned into place, and turned and blind-stitched as you go. The bottom edge could be seamed by hand or machine from the inside, then turned up and the top finished.

Toddler's dress from Mexico, courtesy of Jacqueline Enthoven.

Detail of the dress, showing stitchery and appliqué of bright Mexican cotton.

Detail of an embroidered skirt from Gujarat, India, courtesy of the Costume and Textile Study Collection, School of Home Economics, University of Washington. The border and body of the skirt contain a variety of stitches. Mirror glass is attached by a variety of stitches including *shi-sha*.

Detail of *choli,* or Indian blouse, from India, courtesy of the Costume and Textile Study Collection, School of Home Economics, University of Washington.

Blouse, with design adapted from *choli,* Jacqueline Enthoven. *Materials:* red silk blouse, beads, mirror glass. *Special techniques:* the *shi-sha* glass is attached with beaded thread.

Greek cross-stitched blouse, courtesy of Mrs. Steve Turlis. *Special Methods:* lightly basted seams are further attached with decorative stitches. The cross-stitch was made on a grid of fine mesh, which was later unraveled from under the stitches.

Yugoslavian vest, courtesy of the Costume and Textile Study Collection, School of Home Economics, University of Washington. *Special Methods:* embroidery, partially hidden by large fringe, is almost entirely chain, buttonhole, and herringbone stitches. Below the stitches, a decorative braid has been applied, straight and looped, to form an interesting border.

Vest, Jean Wilson. *Materials:* camel-colored wool, seams joined by chevron-stitch in black wool. Decorative stitches, in a pattern reminiscent of Balkan designs, in white raw silk, copper thread, and black wool. *Special Methods:* sides of vest are laced through embroidered eyelets to close, making it adaptable to several sizes.

Yugoslavian chemise, courtesy of the Costume and Textile Study Collection, School of Home Economics, University of Washington. *Materials:* heavy cotton embroidered in black wool.

Handmade smocked blouse, yoke embroidered by Deb Donaldson. *Special Methods:* the emboidery was worked freely, without predrawing, in the manner of Mexican blouses.

Poncho (also used as wall hanging), Aurabelle Walker. *Materials:* even-weave rayon with suede for circle appliqué and pockets, beads for fringe. *Special Methods:* the design is based on the work of Northwest Coast Indians.

Appliquéd skirt. Maggie Turner. *Materials:* skirt of mediumweight, firm-weave red cotton with the whale appliquéd in a lighter-weight white. *Special Methods:* the whale was inspired by Northwest Coast Indian stylized designs. The elements of such a design make it suitable for using on a large scale.

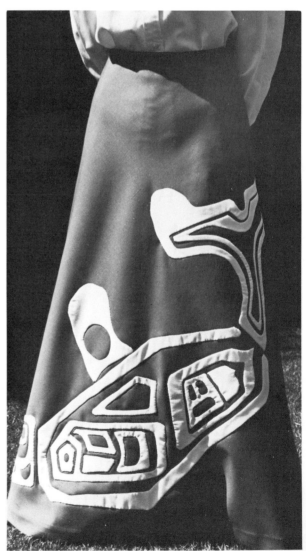

SINGLE-UNIT AND REPEATING-UNIT DESIGNS

Rows of stitches, the simplest kind of design, can make effective borders at hem or neckline, around sleeves, or following seam lines. Try forming a border by repeating a single shape for the length of the border. Then combine several shapes or stitches. Added materials, such as beads, or large stitches with heavy yarn can create texture and interest. Another trick is to gently increase the width of a border design so that finally it becomes quite bold, yet is never overpowering. Such simple projects will help you get started on more elaborate designs for clothing.

A single accent placed on a garment, usually on a sleeve, a collar, or a pocket, can add a personalized touch to an otherwise ordinary item. Placement and size of design can vary widely, but realistic and abstract shapes can both be used. If your garment doesn't have a pocket, add one, already decorated by you.

A single unit can be repeated to form a total design. To repeat a design, it must be marked on the fabric in such a way that the lines can be duplicated. This can be done by counting threads or transferring the drawn design to the fabric as many times as necessary. Measure the length needed for the finished design with a strip of paper. Then fold this strip into sections to work out the size needed for each unit. Mark the design on the fabric if necessary with dressmaker's carbon. Some of the units can be reversed for variation.

The units forming a repeated design need not be identical to be related. Basically all stitchery is linear because the separate stitches are composed of straight lines. Borders use this linear characteristic by building on lines and rows of stitches. These effects can even be emphasized by combinations with appliqué, patchwork, or ribbon. The scale of the individual parts and their rhythmical relation to one another either emphasizes the linear structure or reduces it to create the effect of closed shapes. Lines can flow along to form abstract patterns of their own, and they can lead the eye through or around a design. Repeated designs in borders are quite linear, although the units may be scaled and placed to produce other effects. Consider such different placements as even rows, rows on each side of a garment, mirror-reversed repeats, asymmetrical repeats such as the top of one sleeve and bottom of the other, or repeats along a line that is not straight. Remember that on the body, vertical lines add emphasis to height, and horizontal lines to width. Finally, a design where the stitchery is integrated on a large scale over the whole

Neckline border, Jean Kelso. *Materials:* handmade textured polyester double-knit blouse, embroidery floss. *Special Methods:* a design based on rectangular blocks, each filled with different stitches. The squared texture in the background was a help in placing the stitches regularly.

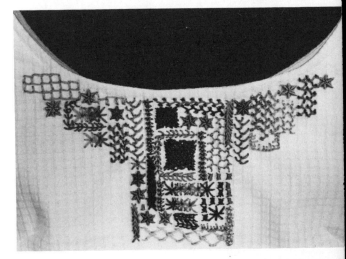

Hem border, Donna Prichard. *Materials:* heavy black yarn is couched on a pale blue wool skirt. *Special Methods:* this is "kinetic art" of a sort! The design, which has no beginning and no end, was dropped onto the skirt, manipulated a little and then secured by couching.

Hem and sleeve border on wedding dress, Aik Kawabata, courtesy of Lynn Pelegruti Haworth. *Materials:* wool crewel yarns and a creamy antique satin, which was used wrong side out to take advantage of the lovely texture and avoid the sheen of the right side.

Detail of the mushroom design on the dress.

Sleeve and skirt trim, Ann Spiess Mills, courtesy of Mrs. Robert J. Young. *Materials:* wool dress, embroidery thread worked in a design suggested by Mexican paper flowers.

Detail of the stitchery on the skirt.

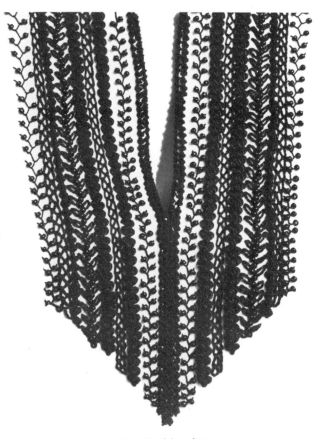

Beaded neckline border, Susan Roach. *Materials:* handmade caftan of a synthetic fabric which is designed to look like a gauzy Indian-cotton weave, black threads of various weights, beads.

Detail of border.

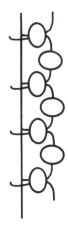

A way to add beads for a border.

Beads can add rich textural interest to stitchery. Detail of patchwork appliqué by Mary Ann Spawn.

Beaded neckline and cuffs, Karin Morris. *Materials:* caftan of seersucker stripe, facings of plain weave on neck and sleeves, knitting worsted, pierced seeds used as beads.

Beaded neckline and cuff borders. Doris Katz. *Materials:* cashmere jacket, old Mexican silver beads, black crochet thread. *Special Methods:* the free-form line was crocheted in a random pattern, and then couched on with chain and squared-chain stitches in colored threads. The jacket was created from an outdated street-length coat. The inside facing at the back neck has a related design for an inside "designer's touch."

Seed pearls with gold metallic crochet threads create an effective medallion out of simple stitches, by Jill Nordfors.

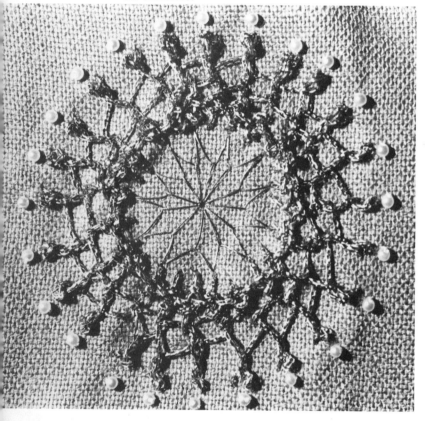

Burro on pocket, Ann Spiess Mills, courtesy Janet Wetzig Collins.

Detail of burro, showing embroidery and needle-weaving on denim.

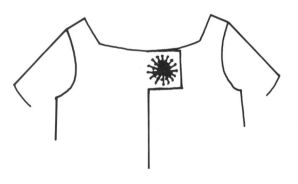

Placement of the medallion on dress.

Lion on center front yoke of child's dress of ticking,
Lassie Wittman.

Geometric repeated-unit design, Phalice Ayers.
Materials: even-weave wool from Denmark, wool
yarns.

Figured repeated-unit design, courtesy of Rilla Warner. *Special Methods:* this Mexican blouse is worked in a stylized bird design (perhaps a chicken) made of closed herringbone-stitches, worked in rows. Tassels are added at regular intervals.

Mirror-reversed design, along curved line, Donna Prichard. *Materials:* skirt is made of melton cloth, heavy yarn. *Special Methods:* the artist manipulated the basic flowing line, pinned it in place when she was satisfied, and copied the design in reverse on the other side. The line was couched into place, then the other parts were added in exact formal balance.

Mirror-reversed design on two pockets of Mexican skirt, courtesy of Betty Hitzman.

Pictures on the following pages:

1
Appliquéd cotton caftan, Jill Nordfors.

2
Detail of caftan, showing needle lace.

3
Dress of white wool with stitchery by Ann Spiess Mills, courtesy of Mrs. Robert J. Young. The design was based on an interpretation of the gaiety of Mexican paper flowers.

4
Appliquéd collar, Gloria McNutt.

5
Dress with arabesque design in appliqué, Gloria McNutt. Photograph courtesy of Jean Ray Laury.

6
Appliquéd silk jacket, Melinda Phillips. Tiny French knots surround each shape of dyed silk.

1

2

3

4

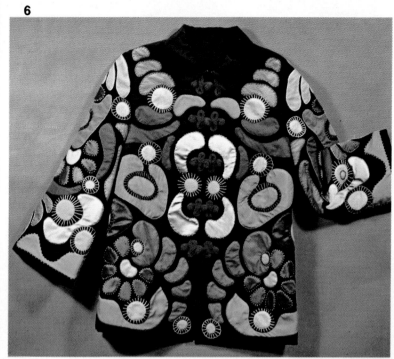

6

5

Mirror-reversed design, on bodice of short caftan, Faye Schaeffer. Courtesy Kathy Schaeffer.

Repeated units do not have to be identical. Appliquéd border on child's skirt from India, courtesy the Costume and Textile Study Collection, School of Home Economics, University of Washington.

Repeated-unit design, Jill Nordfors. *Materials:* sleeveless top is wool knit, with contrasing wool-knit appliqué and varied wool yarns. *Special Methods:* the appliqué pieces were first arranged in a pleasing way, then basted into place. The design in stitchery was worked around and on top of the squares. Then heavy handspun wool was couched on as a running line.

Paisley vest, William Cahill Johnson. *Materials:* Persian wool on linen, buttons made by Mrs. Johnson in petit point. *Special Techniques:* although a traditional design, paisley is a good example of how varied placement adds interest to a repeated-unit design (see drawings on page 74). The pieces of the vest were worked separately before they were assembled. After seaming, the background stitchery was continued, covering all seams. Lining and buttonholes were finished by a tailor.

Detail of the vest, showing varied stitches on a background of Bayeaux stitch.

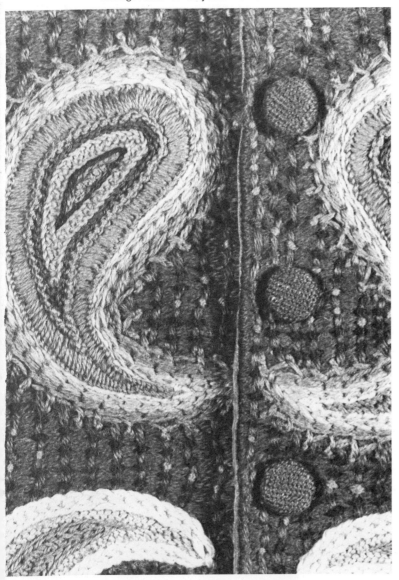

Back of vest. The pattern worked on the Bayeaux stitch repeats the placement of the front shapes, but in different *scaling,* and less ornate. Photos of vest by Fred Figgins.

Variations of scale from one design idea: (1) small accent, (2) small, in repeated border, (3) abstracted so that relative scaling of the parts of the design can be changed, (4) enlarged to become integral part of the garment.

Design of flowing vertical lines, Helen W. Richards. *Materials:* wool skirt, wool yarns. *Special Methods:* squared chain, buttonhole, and featherstitches create a textured, organic effect.

Variations of placement with a repeated-unit design: (1) horizontal row, (2) extended row, (3) row in band, (4) extended-row single unit, (5) variation of extended-row unit, (6) combined horizontal and vertical rows, (7) vertical row in band, (8) separated and elaborated row, (9) continuous repeat, (10) continuous repeats with positive and negative variations, (11) scattered repeats, varied scaling, (12) interlocking repeats.

Caftan by Jill Nordfors. *Materials:* caftan of crisp cotton, appliqués of lighter-weight cotton, yarns. *Special Methods:* a large-scale abstract design of trees is rendered by appliqué trunks and needle-lace branches. Decorative stitches cover the edges of the appliqué.

Detail of needle lace on caftan.

Back view of chasuble.

Detail of shadow stitchery on the organdy circular inset. *Special Methods:* the puckered effect of the background, and the padded effect of the rays from the center wheel are produced by the tension of the running stitch holding the crisp organdy.

Contemporary chasuble, Jorjanna Lundgren. *Materials:* plaid seersucker, organdy and other materials for the inset design, embroidery floss. Photos by Richard Kephart.

MATERIALS
A garment is only as washable or as cleanable as the most perishable fiber used in its construction and decoration. If your material is machine washable, make sure that all lining or interfacings are machine washable, as well as all threads used in stitchery. Boilfast cotton threads are generally safe. To test yarn you doubt, soak it in lukewarm water and then lay it flat, loosely wound, to dry. You can see whether it will run, and, by measurements before and after, how much it will shrink. It is quite possible to use a non-washable thread on a washable garment, but remember that the garment must be handled as though it were made entirely of that perishable fiber. Polyester with silk or wool embroidery must be treated like silk or wool.

Play Clothes and Work Clothes
Be realistic about how much time and expense you invest in stitchery relative to the expected use and life span of the garment you are decorating. It is, sadly, quite possible for the stitchery to last longer than the garment, in which case the embroidered part might be cut out and appliquéd to another item. Play clothes or clothes of a current fad, like denim jeans and workshirts, are fun to stitch on quickly and spontaneously because the doing is more important than the durability. Often such designs are better than serious work—more feeling and joy come through. Use threads or yarns that launder well, as play clothes and sports clothes get soiled frequently.

Katy's Jeans, stitchery by Sandy Bean. Photo by Merry Bean.

White jeans with stitchery by student at University of Washington. *Special Methods:* a large-scale design is made effective with simple satin-stitch, and balanced by a smaller design on the pocket of the opposite side.

Detail of stitchery on pocket.

Logger's workshirt, stitchery by Barbara M. Day. Motif depicts the Ponderosa pine and the creatures of the forests it grows in.

Denim jacket, with stitchery by Joan K. Rave. The
Peruvian motif, done in satin-stitch, shows a running
figure holding a staff.

Appliqué

New bonding materials, frequently meant to be applied with an iron, can be put to good use in appliqué. If the appliquéd piece can just be ironed on, it eliminates turning under the edges before stitchery is added. Ordinarily only non-raveling materials like leather, suede, and heavy velvet can be applied flat, without turning under the edges, but with bonding materials, more flimsy fabrics or loose weaves can also be used. Where the bonding adhesive stiffens the material too much, try cutting only a strip of bonding for the outline of the appliquéd piece. This will leave the large center area unbonded and supple, without making the appliqué less secure.

You can make your own lightweight leather or suede designs quite simply and economically. Commercial use of these materials is often unimaginative and adds much to the cost of the garment, so apply your own pieces, surrounded or embellished with stitchery, to a ready-made suit jacket, vest, or dress. Scraps of many colors can usually be bought quite inexpensively at a leather supplier you can locate in your phone directory. Even a whole skin

Appliquéd trimming, Katherine Gorham. *Materials:* strips of bonded fabric are appliquéd with a shiny material of dyed silk; macramé cord is couched on at the edges.

Appliqué design, Jill Nordfors. *Materials:* suede pieces that are cut and held in place by decorative edging stitches and needle-lace stitches in cord.

Large-scale appliqué, Jo Reimer. *Materials:* various cottons. *Special Methods:* the appliquéd pieces were turned under at the edges and machine-stitched with a zig-zag stitch for a decorative, secure application.

is economical because it supplies so much leather. Working suede and lightweight leather pieces is almost as easy as using cloth because they can be cut with sharp scissors. The cut edge will probably be lighter than the rest in color, and since it won't be turned under, it can be obscured with bulky stitches used next to the edge.

Appliquéd flowers, Aik Kawabata, courtesy Ruth Roberts. *Materials:* crinoline, beads, seed pearls, rhinestones, embroidery floss, metallic thread. *Special Methods:* flowers were first worked on crinoline, using a raised-edge buttonhole-stitch, and then cut out and applied, sometimes with beads, to the background fabric, leaving the petal areas loose for added dimension. Connecting stitchery vines were later worked in stem stitch with metallic thread.

Appliquéd attached collar, Gloria McNutt. *Materials:* bright Mexican cottons. *Special Methods:* although a fairly heavy material was used, the edges ravel, so that they were turned under and blind-stitched. The collar was worked first, then attached to the garment.

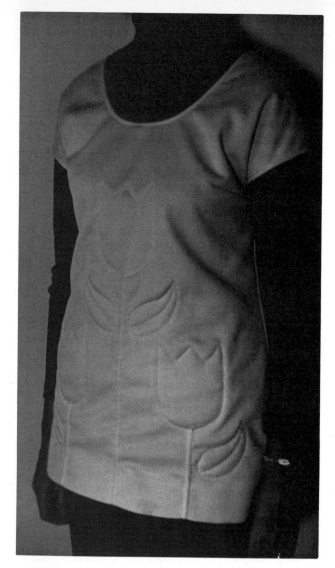

Trapunto overblouse, Geri Douglas. *Materials:* ready-made polyester double-knit overblouse, machine-washable padding, machine-washable lining.
Special Methods: after machine stitching through the three layers—blouse, padding, lining—the padding is cut away everywhere except from the outlined shapes. Then the blouse lining is finished. The batting is secured in this way at the edges of the design to prevent shifting during washing.

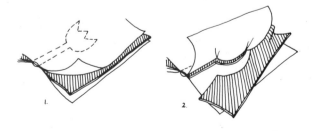

Method used on the overblouse; hatched area is the padding. The stitching can be done by hand or machine.

Trapunto and Canvaswork

Knits are another material with unique possibilities for stitchers. Most of us are familiar with yarn stitchery on handmade woolen sweaters—a natural choice for decoration. Canvaswork and other techniques can also be used with striking effects if you learn to take advantage of the fact that knits do not have a structure of warp and filling threads as woven materials do. They do not ravel quite so easily as woven materials, and therefore can also be used for appliqué without turning under, so long as the edge is secured with stitching. Knits work well for trapunto and quilting because of their stretchiness and resistance to raveling.

The stretchiness of knits makes it advisable to work them with a hoop. You must learn to gauge the tautness of the stitches, because the knits will contract when released, letting the stitches relax somewhat also. On a ready-made garment, lined or interlined areas will be more stable, and a hoop may not be necessary.

Because of the fine yarn and stitches used, modern double knits do not produce high-relief surfaces, but are smooth and flat. A wool double knit is more supple than a similar weight of polyester, which maintains its springy quality. All double knits hold their shape well because of the construction from two strands of a fine yarn, interlocked in a double stitch. When, in the 1960's, a process for using polyester in double knits was developed, the market was revolutionized. See for yourself—the fabrics are widely available at low cost, easily washable, require no ironing, and are easy to sew.

The fine, flat surface of a knit easily takes a pattern drawn on with dressmaker's carbon and worked with yarns of fine to light or medium weight, but it makes heavy yarns difficult to pull through the fabrics. Yarns lie on top rather than blending into the surface, as with the more directional warp and filling of a woven surface.

Canvaswork has interesting possibilities with knits because the canvas can be used as a guide and later removed, leaving the stitches on the knit. (Canvas stitches require counting of spaces, and thus cannot be done directly on knit fabrics.) For this technique it is best to remove some of the sizing from the canvas before using it. Soaking in hot water until the threads soften slightly will take about two or three minutes—the time varies with the material and amount of sizing—but it will shrink the canvas. Soaking in cold water will make it shrink less, and takes about ten minutes. While the canvas is drying on a smooth flat surface, mark your design with a broad-nibbed pen on a sheet of paper. Lay the canvas over the paper, and transfer the design to it—you will be able to see the paper design through the holes—with a waterproof felt-tipped or marking pen. Baste the canvas to the right side of the fabric at the edge of the design, an inch or two outside the design lines. When working on small pieces such as collars and cuffs, it is easier not to cut the pattern piece out of the larger fabric until the stitchery is done.

Pass the needle through both the cloth and the canvas, taking care not to catch the canvas threads. The canvas also serves as a support for the stitching. After completing the stitchery, unravel the canvas by pulling it gently, thread by thread, from the finished stitches. This leaves the stitches directly on the fabric. Any stitch may be used that lends itself to the regularity of the holes: cross-stitch, needlepoint stitches, bargello stitches. This technique can be combined well with insets of ordinary canvaswork on vests, belts, jackets, pockets, or any applied trim.

Canvaswork border on neckline and cuffs by Barbara Johnston. *Materials:* handmade wool-knit dress, wool yarn, needlepoint canvas. *Special Methods:* after the tent-stitch has been worked through both canvas and background fabric, the canvas is unravelled and pulled out from under the stitches. See the step-by-step photographs on page 84.

Jacket with trapunto and Italian quilting, Judy Kasperson. *Materials:* wool double-knit. *Special Methods:* the jacket material and interlining are hand-stitched together along design lines, then the lining is slit at various points to insert padding. Use a lining that does not fray easily so the slits can be closed over with a whipping stitch. Add tacking to hold the padding in place to the edges of the design. After the padding is in place in the major design areas, run yarns through the narrow lines (1/8 inch or so in width) with a blunt needle. This process is called Italian quilting and can be used to form entire designs of lines. *Variations:* use a sheer fabric on top and run colorful yarns through it.

To work canvas stitches on a knit, first cut the pattern shape, without seam allowances, from paper, and work out design on it. On a ready-made dress, also trace the background dress area onto paper before creating design. Then trace the design with marking pen, first onto tracing paper and then onto canvas. Baste canvas into place on the knit, and work needle through both canvas and knit.

When canvaswork is done, unravel canvas from under stitches and pull out the pieces, leaving the stitches directly on the knit.

Detail of finished canvaswork on bodice insert.

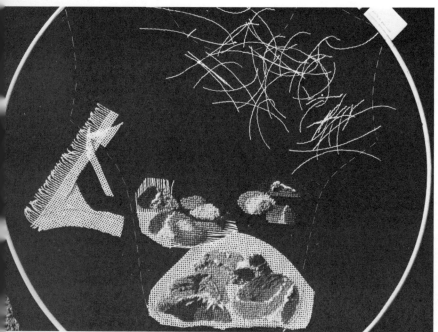

Bargello vest, Elsa Williams, courtesy of Mrs. William Kern. Photo by José Reyes. *Materials:* canvas, Elsa Williams tapestry yarns. *Special Methods:* flame-stitch was worked on canvas marked with the pattern shapes. After working, the shape is cut from the canvas, (with canvas still in place) leaving seam allowance, sewn and lined. Be sure to leave any dart areas free of stitches for later sewing.

Crewelwork, Elsa Williams, courtesy of Mrs. William Kern. Photo by José Reyes. *Materials:* custom-made polyester double-knit skirt, wool crewel yarn, buckram. *Special Methods:* needlework was done through both buckram and polyester, then excess buckram (outside stitching) was cut away.

Detail of the crewelwork on skirt.

Collar trim and belt, Barbara Johnston. *Materials:* handmade polyester double-knit dress, ribbon for belt backing, buckle, wool yarns, needlepoint canvas. *Special Methods:* bargello stitches for the collar trim were worked through canvas and knit, then canvas pulled out; on the belt, seam allowances of the canvas were turned under, and lined with a heavy French ribbon. The edging stitch (similar to leather lacing) was used for a finished edge. The canvas is firm enough to give body to the belt.

Orange collar and cuffs, Elsa Williams, courtesy of Mrs. William Kern. *Materials:* orange sheer silk, needlepoint canvas and yarns. *Special Methods,* pattern shapes were worked on canvas, cut and sewn in as part of the dress. Collars and cuffs usually require stiffening, so that the inclusion of the canvas is functional.

Pink hatband, belt, and trim on pants' legs, Elsa Williams, courtesy of Mrs. William Kern. *Materials:* textured polyester knit, in a waffle-weave pattern, needlepoint canvas and yarn. *Special Methods:* after working, the needlepoint was applied to the pants' legs, and lined and attached at side jacket seams. *Variations:* on a ready-made suit, somewhat similar effects can be achieved by applying all the pieces as appliqué.

Patchwork and Other Techniques

Several stitchery techniques make use of background material which is discarded after being used as temporary support. A variation of patchwork, for instance, can be created to a specific shape for clothing by basting cut pieces to a shaped piece of muslin. Then, after the patches are joined, the muslin can be cut away if the stitches have not been worked through it. In needle lace and needleweaving, stitches are attached to a background only at the perimeter, and may be freed from the background after they are worked. Briefly, needle lace can be compared to knitting and crochet in that it does not depend on a fabric base, but is created from stitches worked into themselves. Many of the stitches evolved from a form of detached buttonhole-stitch that is worked into the row above, forming a lacy, unattached network. Needleweaving, a related technique, consists of using the needle to attach long threads, straight or at various angles, on the fabric for a warp that is filled with any manner of weaving stitches. If pins or small nails are inserted in a shaped support, and warp threads laced or crossed from one pin to another, a small non-loom weaving results. Sometimes this technique is called shaped weaving. Weaving techniques may be worked on any threads that are held at some tension. Jean Wilson's *Weaving Is for Anyone,* and Jill Nordfors' *Needle Lace and Needleweaving* explore these techniques. Mrs. Wilson goes into some detail about stitches that can be used for decorative joining in her book *Weaving Is Creative.*

Patchwork vest, Linda Batway. *Materials:* patches of various materials, satin lining, lightweight muslin. *Special Methods:* a piece of lightweight muslin was cut to the shape of the vest, then "crazy-quilt" shapes were basted onto it at random until the finished shape was reached. The pieces were sewn to one another with decorative joining stitches. See step-by-step photos on page 88.

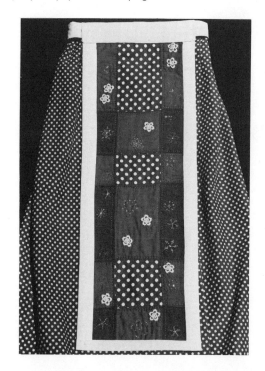

Patchwork panel, Barbara Johnston. The panel, of various cottons, can be hung on the wall when not being used as a decorative panel on cotton skirt.

Detail showing knit pieces being joined with Italian insertion stitch; this joins only the patches, not the muslin. Basting stitches are removed afterwards. When all of the joining stitches are completed, the muslin is pulled free and the yarn ends secured. Only the yarn ends, beginning and ending, go through the muslin, dangling free and unknotted on the back, until pulled free from the muslin.

Finished overblouse, with plain knit back and piping at neckline and armholes, Jill Nordfors.

Patchwork pieces cut to fit an overblouse shape drawn on muslin, then pinned in place. At left shoulder, work has been started on joining the pieces with a needle-lace stitch, after edges have been turned under ¼-inch and basted back (not to the muslin).

Vest (back view), created by shaped, or non-loom, weaving, Barbara Meier. Also shown in color on page 35. *Special Methods:* the weaving was started at the center, creating a series of warp sections out to the edge of the drawn shape.

CHILDREN'S CLOTHES

Children's clothes seem to make non-professional artists relax and do their best work. They are temporary, like sports clothes, because children grow so fast. However, some children's styles are more flexible in sizing than others and can be used for years.

Children not only enjoy doing stitchery but are generally pleased to participate in the creation of their own clothes. Have the child draw directly on cotton with wax crayons, then iron in the design. Use tissue paper over the cloth so wax does not get on the iron. Such a design could be used as decoration without further embellishment except that the colors will fade with washing and disappear with drycleaning. The child's work can become permanent, however, when used as a base for a stitchery design. To do this, reinforce the crayon marks (resist the temptation to add or change a thing) and then you, or the child, can work a free embroidery design over the marks, using the same color scheme. A simple shirt, apron, or tunic makes an easy sewing project, and decorated with stitchery it could not be more special to a young artist.

Dress, Irene Ohashi. *Special Methods:* design for the tree shapes was arrived at by cutting out a paper form.

Smock, Ann Spiess Mills, courtesy of Marlo Medrano and her mother. *Materials:* unbleached muslin, embroidery floss and perle cottons.

Detail of stitchery on dress, showing the variation in pattern achieved by filling each tree with a different object. Note that the center tree is a reversed image of the others, obtained in the folding of the paper shape before tracing.

Portuguese child's smock dress, courtesy of Sabin Kemp. *Special Methods:* all edges except the top hem are bound in bias tape; the large central pocket is embroidered and a drawstring run through the top hem.

Smock dress, shown open. The ingenious, simple design originating in Madeira, allows the dress to be worn full length by a baby, while even a four-year old can still wear it as a top over pants or shorts.

Jumper top, figures drawn by Jill Reimer (aged 5) and embroidered by Jo Reimer, exactly as drawn.

Seashell stitchery on dress for child who collects shells, by the author, courtesy of Kimberly Rush. Photo by Patricia Rush.

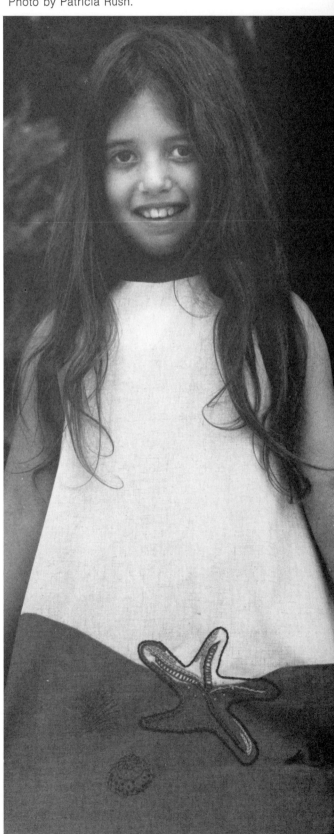

3 ACCESSORIES

Stitchery can be applied to hats, collars, neck-pieces, necklaces, handbags or other carrying cases, and a variety of other personal accessories, for example a watchband of canvaswork. Your imagination is the only limit to inventing variations on the ideas shown here. Instead of a stitchery necklace, try a stitchery pair of earrings or a brooch. Instead of a collar, try the same ideas on a belt.

The clothing and objects to be decorated that have been shown in Chapters 1 and 2 are simple in construction, or else patterns are widely available. With handbags, however, most craftsmen have attempted only the simplest forms. Although some purchased patterns may be obtained with ready-made purse handles, and some instructions are given in books and magazines, this chapter includes many ideas for drafting your own patterns for handbags.

HATS

Hats are not as fashionable as they used to be for formal wear but there is no doubt that they are here to stay. Hats have been worn in various cultures through the ages, often richly decorated with stitchery and attached objects such as beads and feathers. Rain hats, sun hats, and sports hats are common now in most wardrobes, and can be fun to decorate with stitchery in simple or whimsical ways.

Ready-made man's sport hat with crown dots stitched by Pat Albiston.

Handmade hat rings, embellished by Jacqueline Enthoven. *Materials: shi-sha* mirror glass, velvet and grosgrain ribbons, perle cotton.

Ready-made denim sports cap, stitched by the author with rows of Palestrina knot, stem-stitch and up-and-down buttonhole stitch together.

Man's hat from South Africa, courtesy Jean Wilson. *Materials:* machine-quilted cotton. *Special Methods:* small eyelets are stitched by hand with contrasting thread.

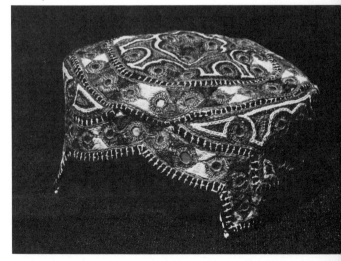

Hat from Pakistan, courtesy Jean Wilson. *Special Methods:* hat is entirely handworked, using the *shi-sha* technique, chain-stitch, and couching.

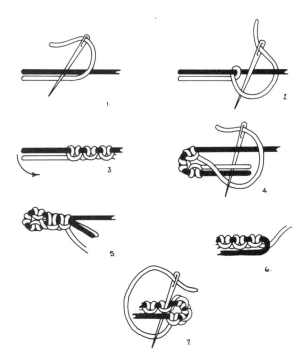

Hat, Egyptian style, Flo Wilson. *Materials:* yarn over linen cord. *Special Methods:* yarn is worked around the cord in up-and-down buttonhole stitch (see drawing). The technique is the same as working on cloth except that the needle goes around the cord instead of through the fabric. *Variations:* heavier rope might be covered in this manner for rugs or constructions of standing shapes. Since the stitches can be spaced apart, other stitches might be inserted, such as Turkey-work for pile. By manipulating the yarn over cording, which can then be coiled, the technique becomes related to one that is used in basketry with different materials.

Above right:
Up-and-down buttonhole stitch worked over cord. Thread a 3-to-5-foot length of yarn into blunt needle, leaving the end of the cord attached to the ball. Hold yarn and end of cord together in left hand (if you work needle with right hand) about 2 inches from the ends of each.
(1) Pass needle up and in front of cord, coming down behind cord, but in front of yarn. Pull snugly. Take needle up and behind cord to right of first loop, coming down in front of cord, but under yarn loop.
(2) Pull taut, and the first stitch is complete. Continue for several stitches.
(3) Fold cord back along itself.
(4) Leave the stitches in the turn of the cord as it is folded. Continue working the stitch over both cords

and the end of the yarn for the short distance they are there.
(5) This catches the ends firmly, and give a finished look at the beginning. If working on thick cord, you might taper the end with sharp scissors, to ease the thickness from two cords to one. By occasionally pulling the underlying cord and pushing the stitches together, your work will remain smoother.
(6) When you have worked the length planned, turn or fold cord back to run parallel with first row. Take needle to the outside and in back of cord, and work two or three stitches from the outside of the curve over the single cord.
(7) After the curve, the stitches continue the same, except that with each pass the needle goes through the loop edge of the stitch above in the same manner with the cord. The stitch may be worked right or left for rows, remembering always to loop your yarn toward the direction you are going. Pull the cording taut occasionally. Continue covering the cord, doubling back wherever needed to create the shape desired.

When a new color, or new yarn, is to be added, simply hold it along with the cord, working the stitches over it for an inch or so. To end your work, repeat the beginning procedure. Cut the cord free from the ball or cone, and fold back along the working cord for the last two inches or so. Work stitches over both, with a single stitch or two at the end to hide the fold if necessary. Run the needle back through the row of stitches for about an inch, pulling the yarn through to hold, and clip.

Brittany bonnet by Jacqueline Enthoven. *Special Methods:* simple shapes are cut out and the seam edges finished with single crochet, done with a fine hook, and then joined by sewing over and over with a decorative stitch.

Two shaped children's hats, Ann Spiess Mills.

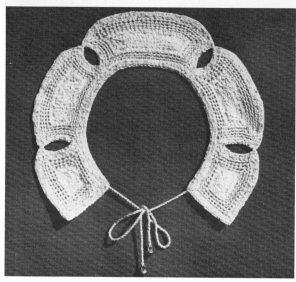

COLLARS, NECKLACES, AND JEWELRY

A detachable collar can solve many problems. It can be made of delicate fabrics and threads while the underlying garment is machine washable or, if the collar is apt to get more soiled, it can be of washable materials while the dress it is worn on, perhaps made of wool, must be more carefully cleaned. Being small, a collar is easy to do stitching on, whereas the large areas of an already assembled blouse or dress are more awkward to work on. A collar can modify the color of an outfit, or put a more flattering color near your face. It can change the dressy or casual look of a garment and be worn on different dresses in the manner of jewelry.

The inside shape of the collar or neckpiece will determine how it fits at the neckline. You can measure this from a dress or blouse you are already satisfied with. The lower edge and outer edges can be widely varied, from a yoke effect, wide at the shoulders, to a thin extension like a man's tie. Fastening can either be at the back or front, or even at the shoulder seam if it can be worked into the design.

Construction of collars varies with the material. The background fabric might be chosen to be part of the design, making it unnecessary to cover the entire surface with stitchery. It is preferable to embroider in a hoop or frame before cutting out the collar, unless a very heavy fabric that provides its own support is used. Frequently collars are entirely faced, and on a simple design, it would be possible to machine stitch the edges from the inside, leaving enough of an opening, either at the back or along the neck edge, to turn right side out. Then a decorative stitch along the edge could be added if desired. Although not as pretty on the reverse side, a soft unlined collar will form to the underlying garment more readily than one with the stiffness of lining added. Consider other methods of fabric construction, too, such as knitting, crochet, or macramé. All of these can be further enriched by stitchery.

The transition from detachable collars to a neckpiece considered as jewelry is only a step. The difference is mainly that the design area of the neckpiece gives the effect of being suspended, rather than drawing the eye to the continuous area around the neck, as in a traditional collar. But there are collar necklaces, too, so the distinction is only academic. Jewelry is always ornamental, rather than functional.

Books or museum collections of ancient jewelry can open your eyes to the unusual materials that can be used for ornamentation—gold and silver are hardly necessary. Stitchery can be used as jewelry in countless ways, as a decorative part of jewelry

Collar, Jacqueline Enthoven. *Materials:* white raw silk and two textured cotton yarns, worked in rows that entirely cover the sheer silk, ties of the same yarns.

Collar in the making. Note that the sheer fabric has been mounted onto a frame. It could also be worked on a hoop. The shape of the collar was drawn directly on the cloth with sharp pencil, but not cut out. After shape is entirely filled with stitches (open rows are Palestrina knots) it is clipped from its base, leaving enough fabric to turn under and blind-stitch. The collar was left unlined for a soft look.

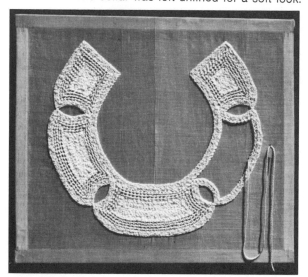

made from materials other than fabric, as part of the support for a large pendant, or as means of attaching a special polished stone or metal piece. Highly ornamental belts, watchbands, and masks are jewelry when their function is primarily decorative rather than useful.

Many jewelry ideas might be started from simple, inexpensive objects purchased at a dimestore. For example, wrapping, stitching, and fringing could transform a plastic bangle bracelet into a work of art.

Shapes for collars: (1), (2), (3), (4) jewel neckline collars, returning to narrow widths for fastening at back of neck; (5), (6) yoke collars, symmetrical front and back, may be fastened at back or sides, (7) Bertha collar, which extends to or just over armhole, (8), (9) mock turtleneck collars, in which the top edge of the collar has been straightened causing it to stand up on neck, (10), (11), (12) neckpieces, with narrowed areas around neck and with suspended, jewelry-like fronts.

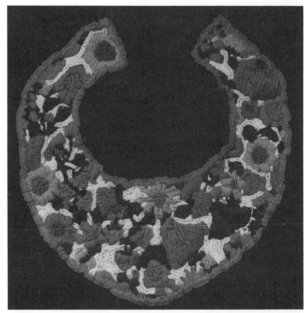

Collar, Jean Munro. *Materials:* lightweight cotton, wool yarn, backing of non-woven stiffening. *Special Methods:* edge is finished by buttonholing.

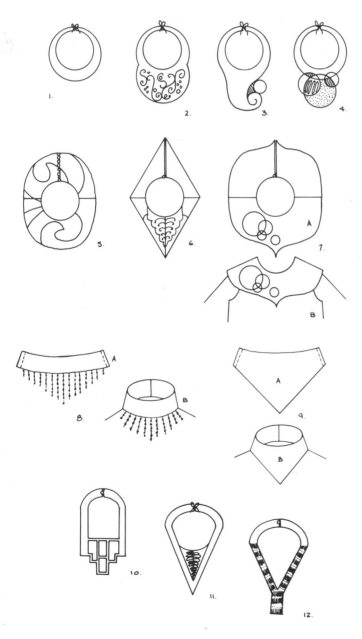

Handwoven collar, Jean Wilson. *Materials:* wool, brooch to fit in shape created for it.

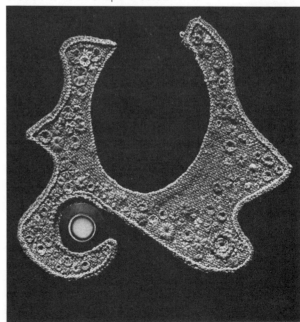

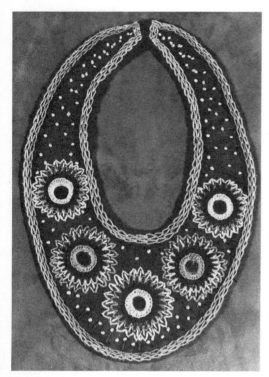

Collar, Irene Proffitt. *Special Methods: shi-sha* attachments, chain-stitch along edge for finishing.

Collar, Pat Albiston. *Special Methods: shi-sha* attachments, decorative buttonhole stitches along edge for finishing.

Collar, Beth Snyder.

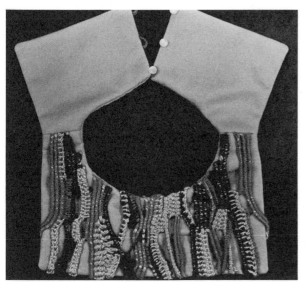

Collar, Jill Nordfors. *Materials:* polyester background, to match dress fabric, various yarns in needleweaving. Collar must be laundered more delicately than matching dress, and is thus detachable.

Neckpiece, Lassie Wittman. *Materials:* neckpiece and pendant of polyester, needleweaving in wool yarns.

Neckpiece, Helen J. Rumpel. *Materials:* wool yarns, bits of silk, glass beads. *Special Methods:* the free-form, needlewoven piece is attached to a knit sweater rather than being tied on like a collar. It can be easily detached when necessary.

Neckpiece, Flo Wilson. *Special Methods:* appliqué and Palestrina knots decorate related units connected with buttonholed bars. The two pieces by Flo Wilson can just as easily be called soft jewelry as neckpieces or collars.

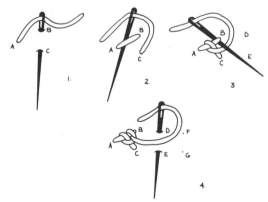

Neckpiece, Flo Wilson. *Special Methods:* appliqué, bead attachments, and Palestrina knots are used to enliven a very simple shape.

Palestrina knot, also known as the double knot-stitch. This is an extremely versatile stitch, which you should try to vary for yourself.

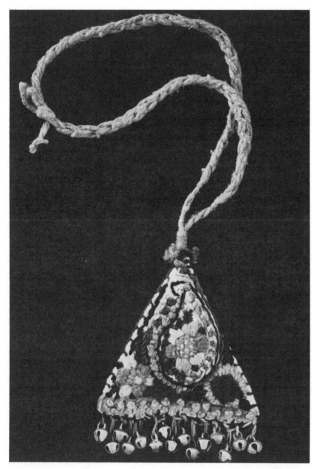

Two necklaces, Pat Albiston. *Materials:* driftwood (on right) combined with padded stitchery in the knotholes; driftwood (on left) mounted on felt, with leather thong and knotted cord for suspension.

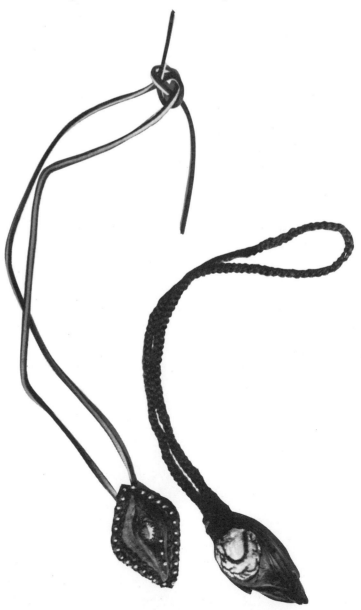

Necklace, Ann Spiess Mills. *Materials:* stitchery on a triangular piece of even-weave dress fabric, braided yarn for suspension, bells as fringe.

Necklace, Norene Firth. *Materials:* plastic lid covered with linen, string, wave-tumbled shells.

Back view of the necklace, showing fringe and suspension-cord attachments.

Necklace, Susan Roach. *Materials:* plastic "ivory" ring, elaborated with string and beads, is hung by a macramé cord of same string.

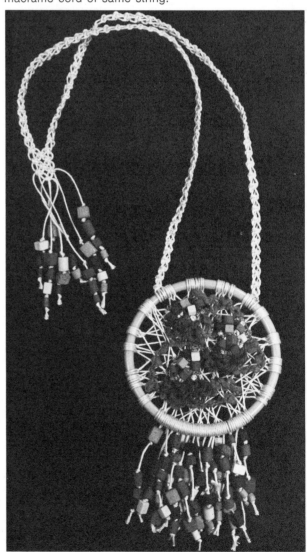

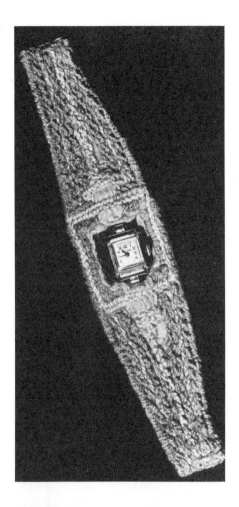

Party mask, by the author. *Materials:* empty eyeglass frames, copper screening, felt. *Special Methods:* the two layers of felt are held on by French knots.

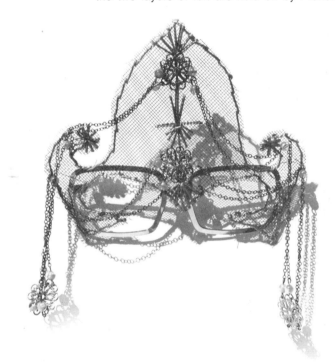

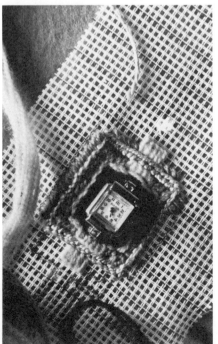

Party mask, by the author. *Materials:* copper screening and "flea-market" necklace mounted on empty eyeglass frames. *Special Methods:* decorative stitchery on screening also attaches the necklace to the frame.

Canvaswork watchband, Jean Wilson. *Variations:* canvaswork can be used as decorative pieces for bracelets, belts, or other accessories.

Detail of watchband being made, showing the simple method of attaching watch and forming stitches. When the band is finished it must be attached to a simple buckle, button, or clasp to hold it on.

HANDBAGS

For a stitcher, planning and constructing a handbag, purse, or pocketbook is a rewarding project, since stitchery shows to such advantage on it. The area to be embroidered is generally small enough so that you can see results quickly, and as an accessory, handbags are less likely to become dated than garments.

Ready-made fabric bags also lend themselves easily to stitchery. If the body fabric has not been glued to the inner stiffening, the bag can be stitched directly, although threads will have to begin and end on the right side of the fabric, since the needle will not go through the stiffening. In that case, cover the ends by working other stitches over them.

Even a leather bag can be embellished with stitchery if you create a panel and glue it on with fabric glue in the manner of an appliqué. On some fabrics, the panel can be blind-stitched into place. Creative possibilities are very wide—consider a handbag as a piece of portable soft sculpture.

Before you draft your own pattern you must consider what kind of bag you want, and for what kind of use. For rugged use, as in a tote bag, beach bag, or book bag, you will need a large-scale bag with a wide opening and strong handles or straps. Materials might be firm cottons, such as sailcloth, ticking, canvas or duck, leathers or plastics, and strong upholstery or handwoven fabrics. The decorations should fit the materials: firm or hand-twist yarns that do not fray easily, secure stitches, or machine appliqués. Strong wools, linens, seine twine, jutes, or nylon cords are appropriate. Consider the ease or difficulty of getting a needle through the fabric in making your choice. Fabrics with rubberized backs might best be avoided for this reason. They can be used if you are willing to wrestle with them.

Use a needle as thick as the yarn to protect the yarn from excess pull. Small pliers can help pull needles through tough fabric. Combine the stitchery with macramé, twining, needleweaving, or other durable techniques, and add only hard-to-break attachments such as stoneware or wooden and bone beads. If the bag is to be washable, do not decorate or line it with delicate or shrinkable materials.

Ready-made bag, stitchery by Nanette Miller.

Tote bag for rugged use, Betty Meisenbach. *Materials:* cotton ticking, perle cotton yarns. *Special Methods:* the ticking was doubled, for strength, and the embroidered front panel was worked separately and attached with stitching, then edges were covered by decorative stitching. Closing is by means of a button hooked under a small flap.

A bag to be used often for general wear should also be relatively durable and resistant to soiling. It will have to be strong enough to wear well when it is slung over your shoulder everyday or left casually around the house. Size will vary according to what objects you want to carry with you most of the time. Fabrics might include upholstery or dress materials, suitings, quilted or patchwork cottons, lightweight to mediumweight leathers or leather-like synthetics. Upholstery or drapery fabrics are usually firmly woven and more durable than dress-weight materials. Leathers should be lightweight, the kind that can be sewn with a long stitch on a machine. Some leathers have been treated to be washable; others can be freshened with a home drycleaning fluid or leather soap.

With any fabric that has a nap, including leathers and suedes, pattern pieces must face the same way, preferably lengthwise. Seams tend to be awkward with any stiff or bulky material, and might be covered with narrow piping, leather strips, yarn ropes, or overlays of stitchery. Yarns for general use might include all the very durable ones mentioned above, as well as firm wools, perle or twist cottons, and linens. Use silk twists, fine threads, and beads as accents among the stronger threads, which will protect them.

A formal bag will be used less frequently, and probably with more care, which means it will seldom need to be cleaned. Consequently you can use the most delicate threads, beads, and goldwork on such a bag. Formal bags are generally smaller than others, carrying only things needed for a few hours, so even very expensive material can be used economically. The most delicate silks, satins, and velvets are strong enough to withstand the infrequent handling the bag will get, but they should be backed for greater stability. Quilting and interlining with muslin, bonding, or other stiffenings, may help support such fabrics. With the new synthetics, things that look fragile may not necessarily be so, and may even be washable, as some brocades and velvets.

Remember that your choice of materials can be greatly extended by using hard-wearing fabrics on the part of the bag that will need them—edges, straps, handles, bottoms—and more delicate or decorated panels for the front, back, and flap of the bag. For example, a leather bag for rugged use could have a central panel of elaborate stitchery done on fabric.

Bag for general use, Mary Ann Spawn. *Materials:* textured upholstery velvet, various yarn. *Special Methods:* bulky seams are hidden by heavy stitching, handle is attached at top sides and self-faced, closing is by means of stitchery-covered cork and loop.

Antique Chinese envelope bag, for formal use, courtesy of Flo Wilson. Being quite small, the bag can hang from a chatelaine.

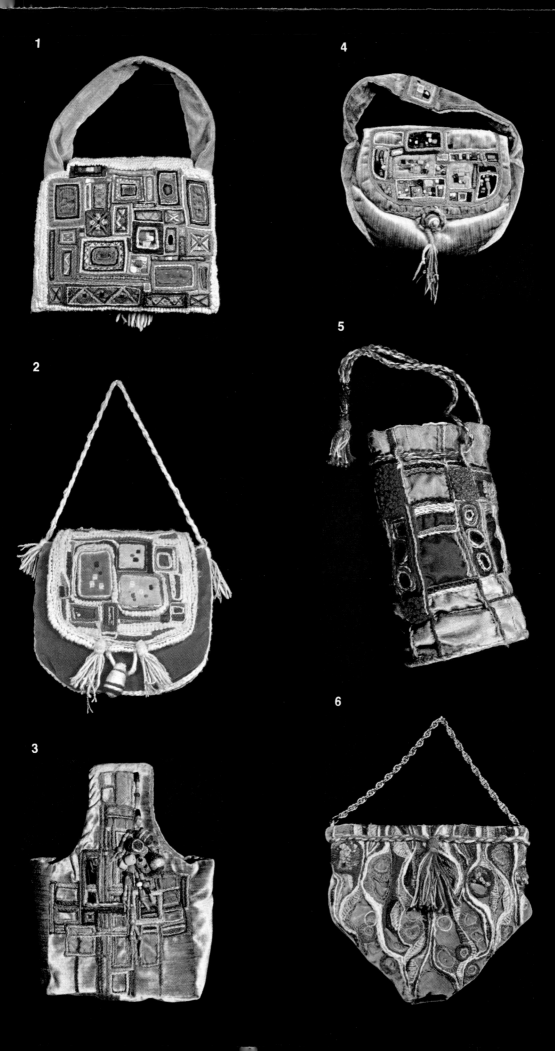

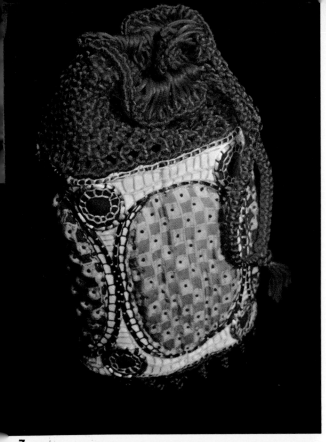

7

10

8

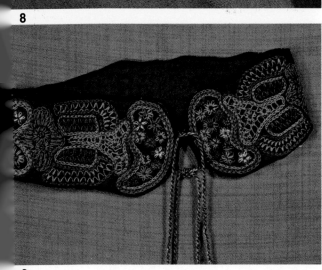

9

11

Pictures on pages 106 and 107:

1

Handbags by Mary Ann Spawn were constructed entirely by her, and frequently employ a patchwork of stitchery-embellished rectangles. Back view of upholstery-velvet bag.

2

Rope handle and needlewoven cork for closing on upholstery-velvet bag.

3

Handle is cut as part of bag shape, and beads and stitchery embellish the velvet.

4

Beads and stitchery on flap and handle of upholstery-velvet bag.

5

Patchwork of decorator's samples of fabric form shaped pouch bag.

6

Free-form stitchery on upholstery-velvet bag with spring-frame closure and chain handle.

7

Macramé bag with panel design of batik and stitchery, Katherine Gorham.

8

Belt of canvas embroidery, by the author. The canvas was partly covered with an applied piece of navy suede and closed with a purchased buckle.

9

Belt of stitchery done on felt, Diane Katz. Two layers of felt, with woven interfacing between, are tied with braids of yarn used for the design.

10

Body Bag, Yvonne Porcella, courtesy of Jean Ray Laury. Suede is covered with needlewoven and wrapped strands.

11

Ceremonial mask, Flo Wilson. Double buttonhole-stitch is worked over ⅛-inch linen cord, in technique related to basketry.

Planning a Pattern

After deciding on the use of the bag, think about the general shape you want: a simple pocket made of a matching front and back piece, an envelope with a flap folding over the simple pocket, a drawstring bag, made from a pocket that pulls shut, or a variation of this basic shape made by adding fullness at the bottom or sides (gussets) or tucking in the sharp corners. Some materials, such as many upholstery fabrics or leather, do not have to have the tuck fastened, as it stays in place by itself. Side seams can be tapered in or outward. Corners can be cut to rounded shapes.

At this initial planning phase, decide what kind of fastenings and handles you want, if any. They are discussed in more detail later in this chapter. Also consider what materials and findings (metal parts such as fastenings, handles, etc.) you have on hand, perhaps as a result of dismantling an old bag.

Cut several shapes from newsprint or heavy paper until one suits you. Simple, inexpensive aids that might be of use are pattern-drafting paper, marked at one-inch intervals, available in some fabric stores, a felt marker, a piece of curved plastic called a French curve, a ruler and a right angle. Cut two of your final shape, without seam allowance.

Now manipulate your cut shapes on a fresh sheet of paper. If there is to be a separate base, cut that; if it is to be a rectangle there will be no difficulty in figuring out how wide the bottom edges of the side have to be to match the base. If, however, your base is to be circular, you will have to make the joining edges of the sides a little more than three times as long as the diameter of the circle, plus seam allowance (see discussion of drawstring bag on page 116). Decide if there is to be a gusset for width, between front and back, and cut two of those. Flaps, handles, or an extension of the side gusset that becomes a handle, can also be cut at this point. Any extra allowances, such as tunnels for holding rods, should also be cut.

Tape all sections together to check your shape, mark notches for matching pieces, and disassemble the shape.

Varying the shape of a bag with gussets. *From the top:* shaped bag, even gusset; shaped bag, tapered gusset; bag with separate base and side gussets; bag with separate base and tapered side gussets. Note that a simple handle can be created as an extension of any sort of side gusset.

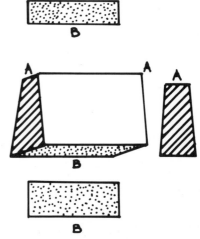

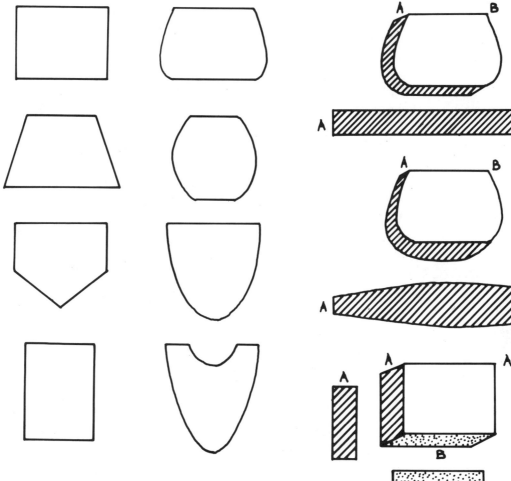

Shapes of bags: the simplest pattern for a bag consists of two matching pieces, a front and a back.

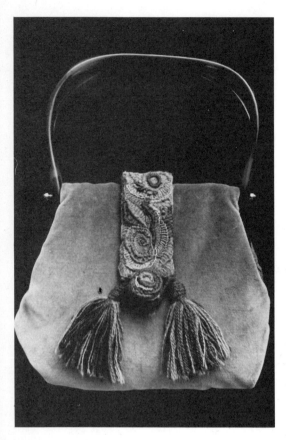

Heavily embellished velvet bag, Mary Ann Spawn.
Materials: gray upholstery velvet, various yarns.
Special Methods: flap has been narrowed to a
strap. It is held by a tasseled loop that fits over a
needlewoven cork (see drawings). Purchased handle
was added.

Reverse of bag, clearly showing the tucked-in area
used for shaping at the corners.

Variations for covering corks: (1) yarn goes *under* two, back *over* one thread (whip stitch), (2) yarn goes *over* two, back *under* one thread, (3) simple over-and-under weaving (warp must be uneven number of threads), (4) detached buttonhole stitch (not built on warp). Making a covered tassel: (1) even lengths of yarn, tied in the middle and doubled, (2) wrapping doubled yarns, (3) buttonhole stitches (any of above methods of needleweaving may also be used). *Variations:* a bead can be pulled over looped area before finishing the top. Padding, cork, or a small Styrofoam ball could be tucked into the top loops of yarn for added fullness.

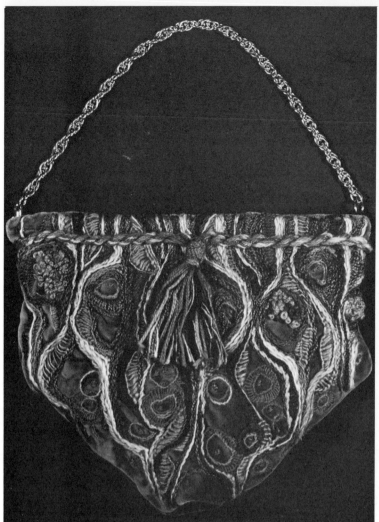

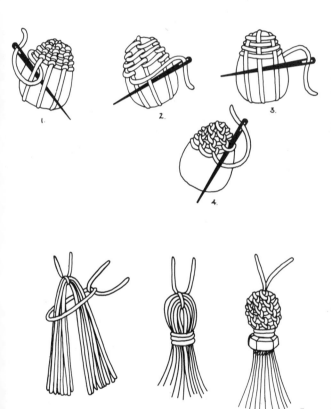

Heavily embellished velvet bag, Mary Ann Spawn. *Materials:* upholstery velvet, various yarns, chain attached by findings to a spring frame, buttonholed tassel. *Special Methods:* the side seams are tapered to a point, but the bottom point has been tucked up to soften the shape. The chain was attached by a professional bag repair shop, as the purchased frame had no provisions for holding the chain.

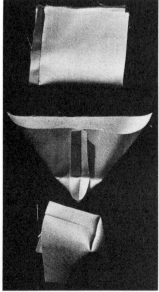

Another shape variation can be created by sewing a seam across the bottom corner at a right angle to the side seam. *From top:* side seam, right-angle seam across it, resulting tuck.

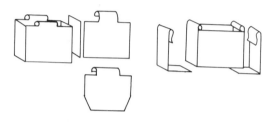

Shapes for separate bases for tote bags or draw-string pouches. When the body of the bag is gathered (as at right) the material for going around the base must be a good deal longer than the normal requirement for going around a circular base (multiply by 3.14). In shapes such as these, it is especially important to try out your pattern measurements by making a paper mock-up.

Extension tunnels for holding rods or handles cut with the shape of the bag. Two variations are shown, for handles attached to front and back, and for handles attached to sides. The extension may also be folded further down to hold a rod below the top edge.

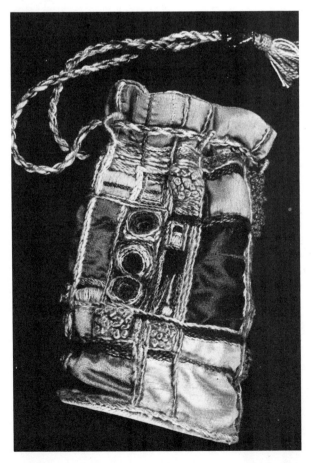

Patchwork drawstring bag, Mary Ann Spawn.
Materials: swatches from a decorator's sample book of ''antique'' satin, rope tie held in place with buttonholed bars. *Special Methods:* artist works by stitching several swatches together, then cuts across them, and rejoins them in different groupings. By rearranging in new directions, her pattern grows. Seams and various areas are embellished heavily with stitches, including French knots and *shi-sha*. See the diagram on page 17.

General Construction

Lay the separate pattern pieces on the fabric you choose, allow for seams, mark for cutting with bast-ing stitches or mark around pieces, but do not cut out if stitchery is to be done on the pieces, since working on cut pieces may fray the edges. Remem-ber to cut fabrics with a nap in the same direction. Handles that continue from one gusset all the way around to the other would have one side with the nap upside down. If this is objectionable, seam the handle at the top, and cover the seam with stitchery.

Does your bag need padding or stiffening as an interfacing? Cut those pieces again from the proper fabric and attach. First, however, you may want to baste muslin to the wrong side of the outer bag material to add to the firmness as you embroider; the needle goes through both layers.

Interfacing should be added after any embroidery is done and after any snaps or closings are sewn on. If the interfacing is to be ironed on, make sure to protect the stitchery by placing the stitchery face down on a terry-cloth towel, and ironing on top of the piece. Applying the stiffening only to the seam line makes for less bulky seams. A double layer of interfacing along the outside edges of any flaps will add definition and strength to a part that gets much use.

Padding, such as dacron, is also too bulky to seam, so that it can be cut about half-an-inch short at the edges, and basted to the wrong side of the purse pieces. Later, when they are joined, the padding will butt together.

After the inner layer is attached, the next step is to sew the bag together. Piping may be added to the outside seams. It can be a narrow strip of fab-ric, frequently cut on the bias for flexibility, or of leather, folded over cording and stitched into the seam with a zipper foot. It is easiest to machine baste the piping to one side of the bag, then put the joining piece into place and stitch through all four thicknesses. The zipper foot allows you to stitch close to the cording, but hand sewing can be

Inside lining of the patchwork drawstring bag. Note that the lining is attached only at the top edge, and that the base of lining has been cut and attached separately just as on the outside. An interesting touch here is that the lining is also made of patchwork.

done, too. An attractive alternative to piping is covering the outside seam with stitchery at a later point in construction. Flaps that are not cut as part of the back piece will have to be sewn on at this point. Special instructions are given for construction of different types of bags on this and the following pages.

If the bag is to be lined, cut and seam the lining pieces slightly smaller than the pattern pieces, to allow for the thickness of the interlining. Use light or mediumweight fabric which can both add body and withstand the wear and tear that the inside of a handbag gets. Dress fabrics are probably too soft, but they can have iron-on interfacing added to the wrong side of the lining before it is sewn together.

Add pockets to the lining pieces. There are several methods of doing this, but they are all variations of patch pockets, being tacked to the lining rather than sunk in it as for a coat pocket. A large pocket can be divided into several compartments with additional seams. The following is one method: cut a square of fabric double the finished size plus seam allowance. Fold in half, wrong side out, and sew the side seams only. Turn and press. The open end may be overcast to prevent fraying, if desired. Lay the seam line of the pocket along the *bottom* edge of where the pocket is to be placed, with the pocket extending *down* from this line. Stitch along the seam line. Fold the pocket upward into place and press, then stitch the edges. Be sure that the bottom corner edges are cut or tucked inward under the stitching.

Now sew the lining pieces together and turn right side out. If your bag material is thin, you may be able to sew the lining and the bag together at the same time, which tacks the lining in place. If not, sew the assembled lining to the bag with a blind-stitch or decorative stitch.

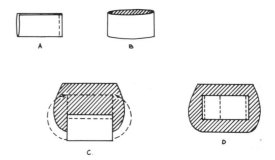

One way to make an inside pocket attached to lining: (a) fold fabric double, and sew side seams, (b) turn right side out, and press, (c) lay the seam edge of the pocket along the bottom line of where the pocket is to be placed, and stitch, (d) turn pocket up and sew edges in place. Additional seams may be added for dividing the pocket into sections.

Envelope Bags

This common form of bag may be thought of as a rectangular pocket shape with a flap. It may or may not have gussets and a handle, but a prominent flap is what gives it its name, as it looks like an envelope. Basically only one pattern piece is needed for an envelope bag without gussets—a rectangle that can be folded in thirds to form the proper shape. The bottom third matches the center third and the two are stitched together at the side seams. The top third is folded over as a flap, and may be of a different size or shape from the two sections that form the bag. If side gussets are used, the pattern is folded in the same way, but the top flap and the bottom must be increased to span the width of the gussets as they fold over them.

Many envelope bags need stiffening to hold their slim, tailored shape. Fasteners can be hidden under the flap or used prominently on it as functional decoration. Perhaps all that is needed as fastening is a button and a twist of yarn on the flap to catch the button in. Slim handles, if any, are suitable. A simple one can be formed from a yarn rope or chain attached at the sides of the bag. And old-fashioned but attractive way of holding such a bag is a chatelaine, which can be clasped to an article of clothing or hung from a belt.

Burlap book bag, Russell Veles, aged 8. *Materials:* burlap, various weights of yarn for braided rope handle and decorations.

This simple bag is created from a single rectangular piece. Fringed edges eliminate seam finishing. The stitchery design, which includes couched-on yarns, is done before the sides are seamed, with the support of a tacked-on frame.

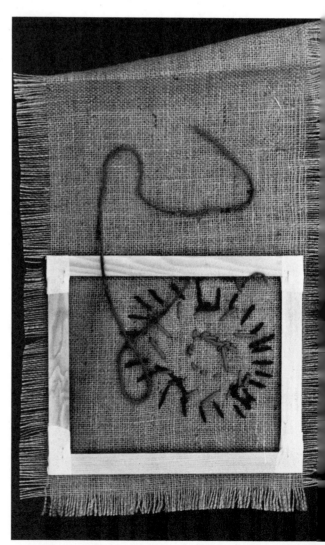

Variations on the basic envelope bag involve varying the shape of the flap. When the shape of the body is changed, it no longer is a classic envelope bag, although construction follows the same principles.

Envelope bag, Jo Reimer. *Materials:* wool, wool yarns, lining material in paisley print.

Drawstring Pouches

The simplest pouch bag can be created from a single rectangle folded in half, seamed at the sides, and hemmed at the top to form a channel for the drawstring. If a more stable shape is desired, a separate base piece can be added, usually but not necessarily a circle. The pouch bag can vary from the sailor's duffle bag to delicate evening bags just big enough for a few small items.

To make a separate base, cut a circle of the proper size from a plastic lid. Measure the diameter (widest distance across) and multiply that times 3.14. The resulting number is the length of material you will have to cut to go around the circle (circumference), and it does not include seam allowance. Sometimes a pouch bag is gathered at the bottom where the material for the sides is sewn to the base. In that case, you will have to allow more length for take-up. The height of the material is up to you; however, you can save yourself a step (when using lightweight fabric) by cutting twice the desired height and folding the material so that the bag is ready lined. Do whatever interlining and stitchery you plan, and then sew the side seams and gather the bottom edge.

Now cut a circle of fabric from the plastic base form, adding seam allowance. Sew the bottom circle into the tube of fabric, and turn the shape right side out. Put the base piece in, and glue it lightly in place with fabric glue, unless you are sure that the lining material will hold it firmly.

If the lining was not included by doubling the fabric, cut and sew a separate lining in the same way as the outer shell, and blind-stitch at the top edge. If the bag is to be hemmed at the top, perhaps for a drawstring, then the lining would extend under the bottom edge of the hem, to be seamed with the hem.

The drawstrings may be of any fabric, rope, or cord strong enough to withstand the constant friction caused by opening and closing the bag. Do not use frayable material. It is possible to use two cords, each pulling in the opposite direction. If a hem is not desired, use eyelets cut into the bag, or rings, large beads, or buttonholed loops attached to the outside. Anything will serve that allows the strings to pull.

Drawstring pouch, Jacqueline Enthoven. *Materials:* silk-like polyester, lightly interlined, boilfast cotton perle yarn, *shi-sha* mirrors. *Special Methods:* bag is gathered on a separately covered circular base. The mirrors are surrounded with a variety of stitches. The side piece was cut long enough to gather to the finished measurement.

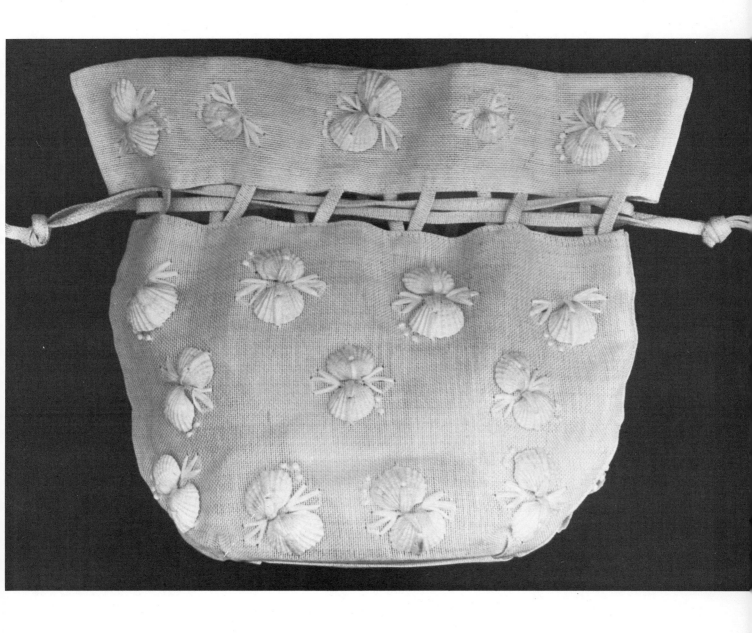

Drawstring purse from the Philippines, showing two drawstrings that pull in opposite directions. Courtesy of Jan Grant.

Handles, Fastenings, and Tassels

Handles may be made of the same fabric as the bag, and attached to one of the pattern pieces. They may be separately constructed of other soft materials such as leather, cord, or fabric, or they may be purchased chain, plastic, and metal handles, perhaps with hinged purse frames and snap fasteners attached. Consider attaching a handle system from a bag you no longer want to a newly made and decorated one.

The kind of use the bag gets will affect the placement of the handle. A small clutch might safely swing from a single decorative strap in the center or at one side, but bags large enough for general or rugged use must support a reasonable weight and be in a comfortable balance when suspended from arm or shoulder. A single handle, short or shoulder length, can be placed at the top of the sides, but double handles are placed somewhere on both front and back.

A handle that is an integral part of the bag, such as a continued gusset strip, or a continuation of

Bag with handle cut as part of the shape of the body, Mary Ann Spawn. *Materials:* upholstery velvet, beads, yarns, lining material of lightweight but firm drapery fabric, interlining of dacron padding.
Special Methods: a single gusset adds fullness to bottom and sides.

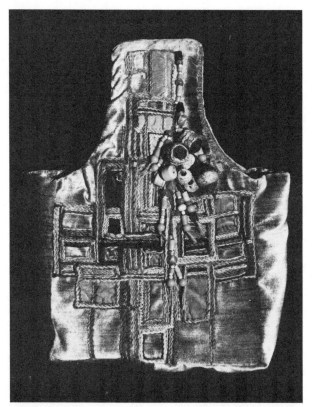

Shape variations for bags that include handle as part of the bag shape.

the shape of the bag itself, will be of soft material, whose strength might be increased with interlining or with reinforcing surface stitches. When the gussets are in one piece with the handle, the handle section will have to be lined separately. This can be accomplished in one of two ways. Lining can be allowed for during cutting by leaving one-half of the width, plus seam allowance along each side of the handle length. The finished handle would then be self-faced and have a single seam underneath the center. Alternatively, a separate lining piece can be cut the same shape but slightly narrower than the handle, and the seam sewn along each edge of the fabric. If the handle area is not a straight shape, this method must be used. In either case, line, interline, then turn the handle right side out before sewing the gusset sections.

To make a fabric handle which is attached to the bag later, measure the length of the strap, plus attachment allowance. Cut double the width, plus seam allowance. Add any stitchery. Reinforce the full piece with one or more layers of iron-on interfacing, unless the fabric is exceptionally firm and strong. Cut muslin or dacron padding for interfacing. Lay this on the wrong side of the fabric, fold lengthwise, and stitch. Trim excess interfacing as close to the seam as possible. Press the seam open and turn right side out. Blind-stitch or otherwise finish the ends, and attach.

Ropes and wrapped cords are also good for handles, and merely have to be attached firmly to the body fabric. They may be made any length, and can also be used for belts, ties, suspensions for necklaces, or couched onto fabric as ornamental trim. A flat strap or rope big enough to be used in a single width may be covered with yarns in varying colors. Wrap or wind the yarn around the strap tightly, and secure the ends by weaving back under the wrapping. If covering with stitchery, the knot of the plain buttonhole-stitch or up-and-down buttonhole-stitch will make a pleasing pattern. If the stitches run to the end of the rope without further finishing, a small dot of glue will secure the end stitch. A combination of stitches, as well as colors, can make the piece interesting.

Mini-bag with rope handle, Mary Ann Spawn. *Materials:* upholstery velvet cut approximately to 2½ x 3½ inches, yarn rope with fringes left at ends. *Variations:* see drawing for method of making a twisted rope (page 121).

Bag with ribbon handle, Barbara Day Taylor. *Materials:* the body of the bag is created from ribbons machine-stitched together and embellished with stitchery. *Special Methods:* handle sewn directly to the inside of the bag.

Detail of tassel. A connecting loop, covered with buttonholing, was slipped onto the tassel threads before they were covered with wrapping.

Detail of wrapped handle, showing underlying nylon strap.

"Body Bag", Yvonne Porcella, courtesy Jean Ray Laury. *Materials:* suede, yarns for all needlewoven trim, pocket, tassel, and wrapped handle. The handle is a nylon strap.

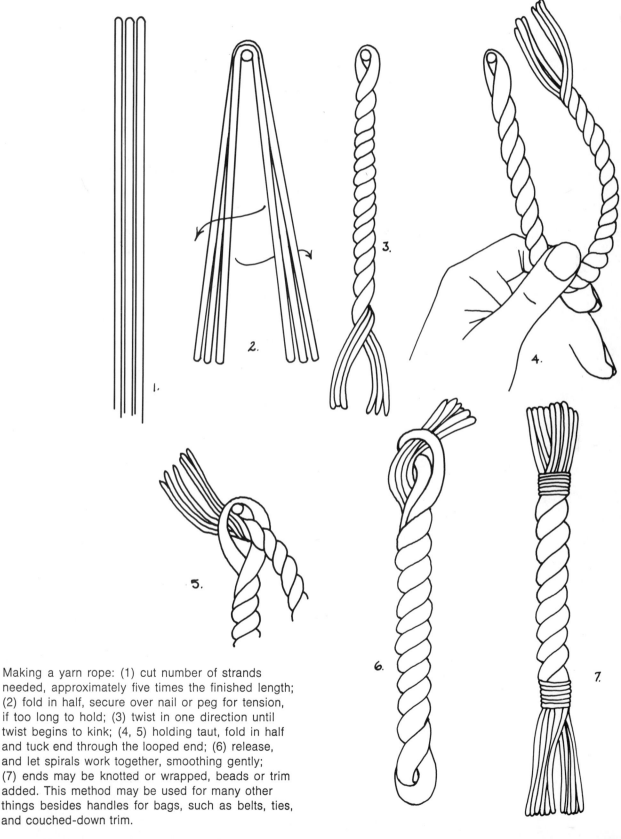

Making a yarn rope: (1) cut number of strands needed, approximately five times the finished length; (2) fold in half, secure over nail or peg for tension, if too long to hold; (3) twist in one direction until twist begins to kink; (4, 5) holding taut, fold in half and tuck end through the looped end; (6) release, and let spirals work together, smoothing gently; (7) ends may be knotted or wrapped, beads or trim added. This method may be used for many other things besides handles for bags, such as belts, ties, and couched-down trim.

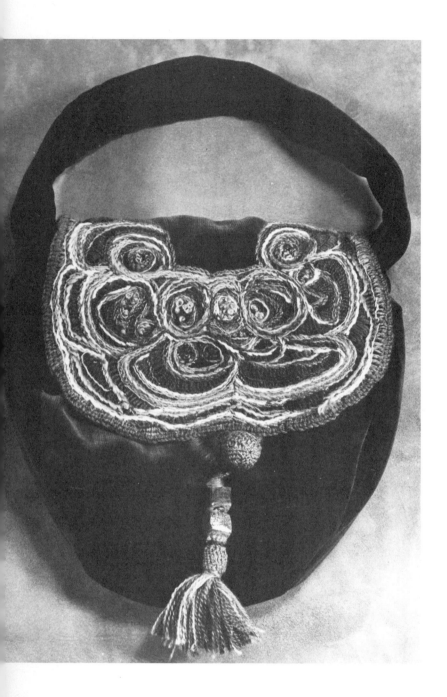

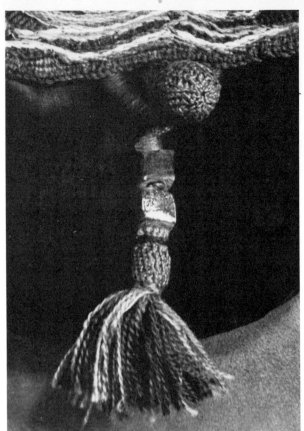

Detail of the covered cork and wrapped loop closing. The loop has been decorated with an elaborate fringe. Two beads have been pulled over the loop onto the wrapped area.

Shapes for bags with gussets and handles in one piece: (1) gusset with extra width for lining handle area; side extensions are folded to center and seamed; (2) gusset-handle with separate lining piece (this method must be used if handle is not a straight shape), (3) gusset-handle as extension of sides of bag, with separate lining piece.

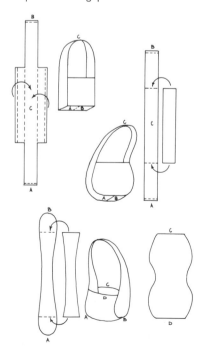

Envelope bag with handle formed by extended gusset, Mary Ann Spawn. *Materials:* upholstery velvet, yarn for stitchery and covering cork on tassel and knob, dacron padding for interlining (including flap and handle). *Special Methods:* gusset cut to be self-lined in handle area (see drawing); flap stitchery consists of stem and Palestrina stitches pulled so tightly in circular forms that they produce concave areas for added dimension.

Non-fabric handles may be attached in a variety of ways. Chains may be couched directly to the bag, inside or out. Some purchased handles have a frame that is fastened directly to the bag by sewing through small holes in the frame. Like drawstrings, some non-fabric handles run through hems or fabric tunnels. These tunnels are strips of material sewn to the bag except at the open ends. They may be on the front or back, or on each side; they may extend above the top edge of the bag or be sewn along the inside top hem. If decorative, they may be put on the face of the bag in front and back. If the body material is flexible, the tunnel itself may be gathered on the rod. Many purchased handles are crafted so that a rod, attached to the carrying handle, goes through a tunnel. There is no reason

Variety of purchased snap-lock and hinged frames, courtesy Phalice Ayers.

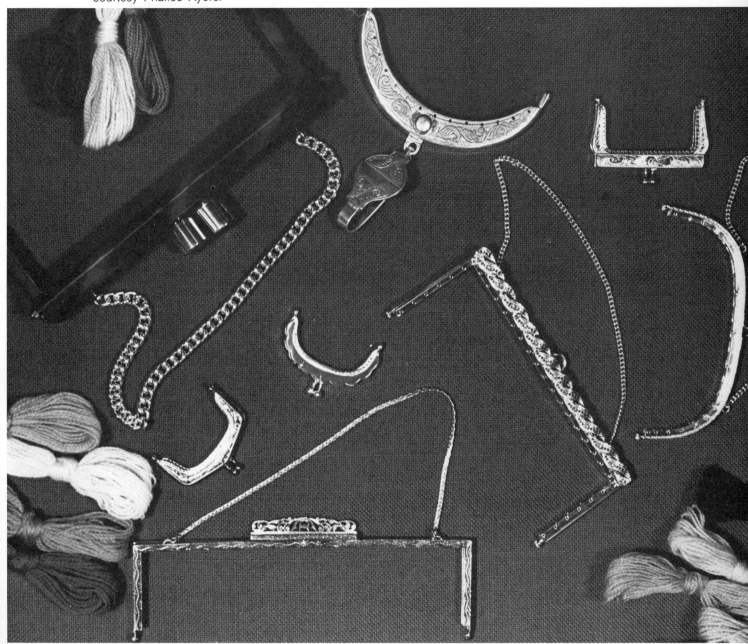

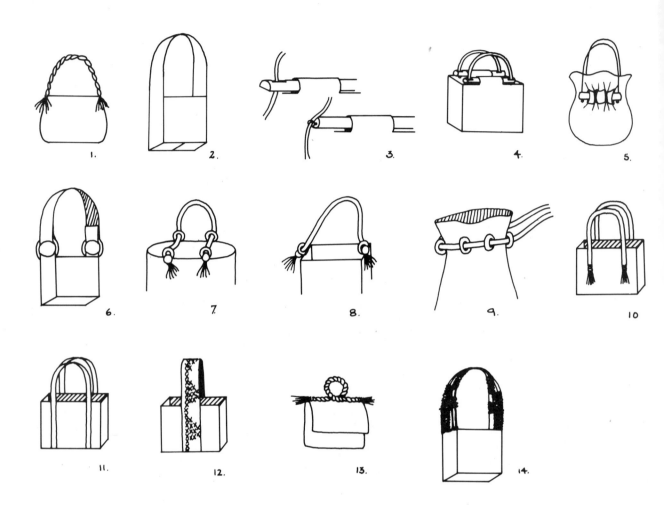

why you cannot create your own rods from lengths of dowels, and attach either fabric or non-fabric handles to them by tiny screw eyes at each end of the dowel or holes drilled in the ends.

A carrying handle or rod can be run through rings or loops sewn on the surface of the bag, like curtain hooks. Rings at the side can also be attached at each end of a simple strap. Any ring, even a discarded plastic one, can be buttonholed or wrapped with yarn for an attractive effect.

Decorative purse handles and frames are available in many styles and prices. Lovely old antique frames can be found on old bags and reused with new fabric. Examine how such an old handle is attached to the fabric before you buy it, as that may limit the materials you can use. For example, if the handle must be sewn on, you will not want to try to apply it to a thick fabric. If there is a hinge or base area on the frame, notice how far it allows the bag to open. This, more than the top opening, determines the amount of access room to the bag, unless added to with gussets.

Some handles and frames require professional mounting. Usually this involves rods or attaching holes that must be reached with special tools, or application of linings and interlinings that require special skill. There are professional services available in many cities, or by mail order, to which you send the embroidered fabric for all the necessary parts and services, generally including lining. Your local yarn shop or a needlework magazine will be able to supply addresses for these services, which are usually expensive.

Opposite:

Variety of handles that can be made: (1) rope attached to each side, (2) handle cut as part of gusset, (3) detail of dowel end, one with slit hole for handle to thread through, the other with a screw eye at the end to attach a rope or chain, (4) dowel through tunnel holding shaped handle, (5) tunnel attached to surface of bag, and gathered onto dowel for attaching handle, (6) large rings, connecting bag and handle, (7) rings for threading rope to draw closed the front and back, (8) small rings on edge of bag for threading rope through, (9) small rings on surface of bag for drawstring, (10, 11, 12) handles attached to bag surfaces, (13) heavy cord or rope, looped for handle and attached with wrapping or up-and-down buttonhole stitch, (14) three cords attached at ends, connected and strengthened by needleweaving.

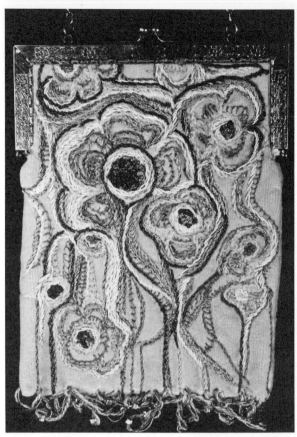

Home-mounted bag, Mary Ann Spawn. *Materials:* silver frame and handle found in antique shop, upholstery velvet, perle cotton, washed silver thread, gun-metal beads.

Home-mounted bag, Mary Ann Spawn. *Materials:* imitation tortoise-shell handle that contains a rod that slides into a fabric tunnel, upholstery velvet, tie-dyed silk tucked in with rows of stem-stitches and bullion-stitch clusters, various yarns.

Professionally mounted bag, canvaswork by Barbara Day Taylor. *Special Methods:* the used, worn fabric was removed from antique filagreed frame and used as a pattern for the canvas. The pattern repeat was chosen to match the large green stones of the frame, both in color and size.

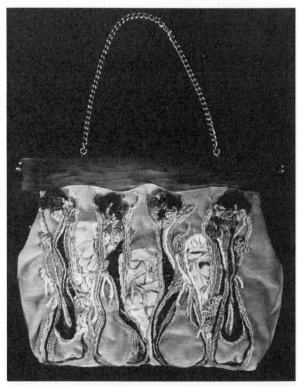

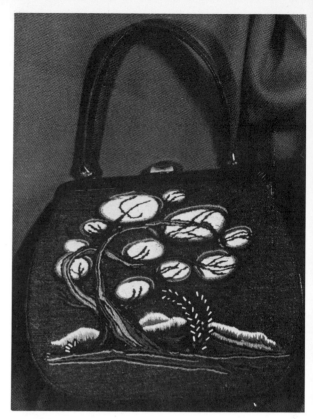

Professionally mounted bag, crewel embroidery by Dorothy M. Chapman. The worked material was sent to a mounting service, where bag was lined and finished.

Home-mounted bag, Mary Ann Spawn. *Materials:* purchased bamboo handles, cotton print in log-cabin quilting design, velveteen panel with cotton appliqué and stitchery, large paillettes attached in the *shi-sha* manner.

Home-mounted bag, designed by Nancy Hegg, worked by Phalice Ayers. *Materials:* purchased metal handle-frame on a chatelaine, canvas, needlepoint yarn. *Special Methods:* frame is stitched directly to the fabric through a row of small holes in frame.

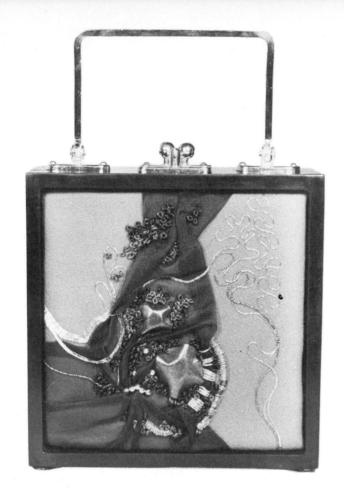

Home-mounted bag, Virginia B. Carter. Photo by James B. Carter. *Materials:* unfinished wood box with recessed top, findings including hinges, snap fastener, handle, lining material, fabric panel of wool crepe, chiffon, gold-finished kid, silk thread, gold and Japanese gold threads. *Special Methods:* the decorated wool panel was padded and mounted on cardboard to fit the recessed top, then glued into place.

Basket purse, embroidered panel, handle and flap decorations by the author. *Materials:* purchased basket, linen, yarn, mat board, padding, beads. *Special Methods:* the stitchery on linen was padded and mounted on mat board cut to fit over the wooden basket lid. A bias strip of linen is held in place over the lid edge with fabric glue and threaded lacing. In this way, both the decorative panel and the lining piece come just to the finished edge. The handles were padded with strips of yarn that extend for tassels, and covered with yarn worked in the up-and-down buttonhole stitch. Fastening is by means of suede strip cut over two pieces of deer horn tied on by a yarn rope.

Fastenings can be bought or made. As mentioned, a simple button attachment may be all that is necessary for an envelope bag. A large snap on the inside of the flap will also do. Look at the pictures in this chapter to see what kind of variations on closings you can invent for yourself. Some of the fastenings shown here can be used on many types of garments as well as on bags.

Fastenings function to join two parts together. One side generally receives and holds a projection from the other side. Buttonholes, eyelets, loops, bars, or ties may join to anything that will hold its shape firmly: hooks, knobs, beads. Ties may be of braid, cord, rope, or lacing.

Stitchery can be used in two ways on fastenings —either as a functional part of the system—a looped stitch, for example, might go over a bead— or as an embellishment to the existing fastening. Buttons, which may be made of many decorative materials such as bone, clay, wood, and beads, can also be corks covered with decorative needle-weaving or needle-lace stitches. Tassels can be covered, and may serve more than a decorative function, as they can often solve the problem of how to finish off dangling ends of yarn. The tassels may also be part of a fastening system if they are the correct size to slip through a matching loop. Loops, which should be of firm materials or have several added strands of durable material like nylon cord or fishing line, because they get much wear, can be decoratively covered with stitches or formed from decorative ropes of yarn. The buttonhole stitch and up-and-down buttonhole-stitch are handy for covering although they do not by any means exhaust the possibilities. The stitches can be extended onto the background fabric to hide the attaching ends of the loop.

A loop can be formed of a full circle, too. Try attaching one of the flexible rings that hold six-packs of soda cans, or a ring cut from a plastic lid, and then embellish it with stitchery.

Decorative trim incorporating button loops, Susan Roach. The trim is worked in Palestrina knot as couching over a fine cord, which continues on the cord (but free of the background) for the loop.

Decorative eyelets with braid ties, worked in with decorative surrounding stitchery, Diane Katz.

Beads used for lacing are caught in the second row of Palestrina knots at regular intervals, Susan Roach.

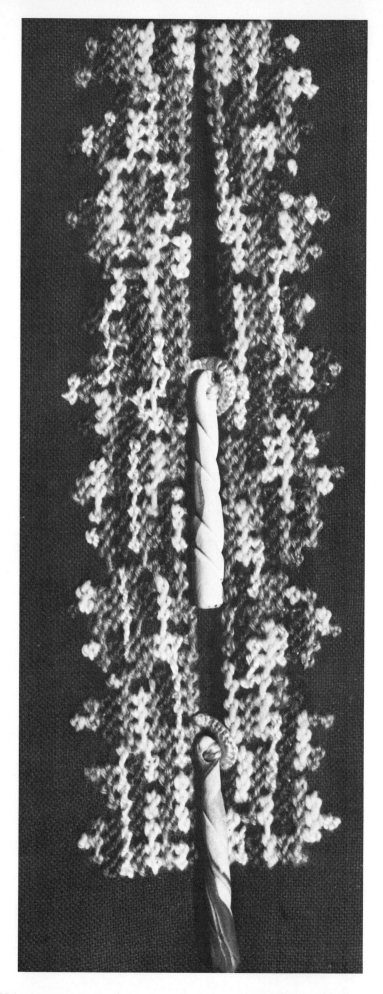

Decorative opening worked in raised chain band in wool over linen threads (see diagram), in colors to match clay twists used as buttons, by Susan Roach.

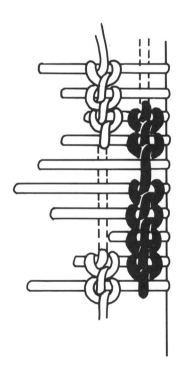

Detail of the raised chain band, showing the distribution of the different yarns.

Opposite:
Cork shapes for covering, with needleweaving started on one. Fishing corks are good for this purpose because they have a hole in them, but any cork can be used by piercing a hole through the center. The warp can then be threaded through the hole, down the outside, and then back through the hole. This step is repeated until the threads are spaced at a workable distance apart, and ending with an uneven number. Use lightweight yarn or cord to allow enough room for all the warp necessary. To use heavier cords pull as many strands through the hole as will fit, weaving a short distance, and then adding more warp yarns by attaching to the woven threads.

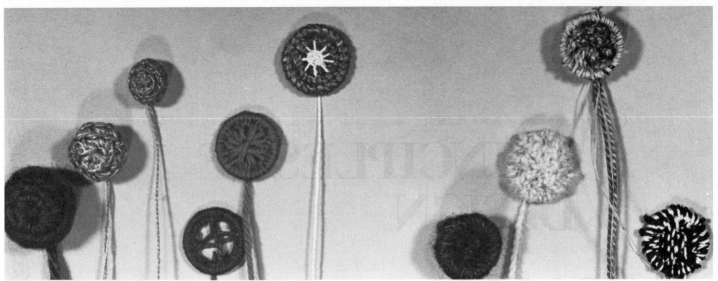

Series of buttons worked from bone rings, Mary Hanson. *Materials:* bone rings, various yarns including perle cotton, crochet thread, raffia. *Special Methods:* the first series of three (at left) are various weights of thread worked continually around rings in single crochet, allowing a ball shape to form. Excess yarn is stuffed into the cup shape, then closed on the back with several stitches, leaving a long enough end for attaching. The second series of three (in middle) are covered with buttonhole-stitch, with the loop edge toward the center. Threads can then be attached to loops for weaving, or left as spokes. The third series of three (at right) uses the blanket-stitch on the ring, continuing it as a detached stitch until a cup shape is formed. The cup can be turned inward or outward, filled or stuffed for added effects. The button at lower right has threads attached into the blanket-stitched edge as a warp, and then woven.

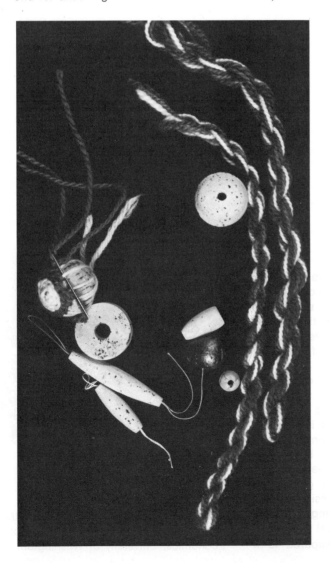

Loop and covered-cork closing, with tassel added to the loop for decoration. The tassel form has been filled out with padding. The knob is covered with buttonholing as well as needleweaving, and the loop is wrapped.

4 ELEMENTS AND PRINCIPLES OF DESIGN

ANALYZING DESIGN

Usually new stitchers are too critical of their work. They try to turn out a product of museum quality instead of taking their clue from the informal, simple joy of folk art, which is art worked at home to be lived with and used. A characteristic of folk-stitchery, even that from very primitive cultures, is the simplicity of stitches, used freely and rhythmically.

Perhaps our culture has been too content to accept quality of design as completely subjective, which gives stitchers the idea that if they don't have "born talent," they can never succeed in learning the principles of design. However, even a person who "doesn't know a thing about art, but knows what he likes" can learn to follow general guides to design, and improve his work. These guides are not deep mysterious secrets of professionals, but ideas distilled through centuries of trying to understand and appreciate all forms of visual art.

Basically, good design can be compared to a

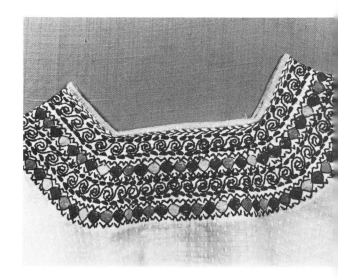

Blouse from Guatemala, courtesy of the Costume and Textile Study Collection, School of Home Economics, University of Washington.

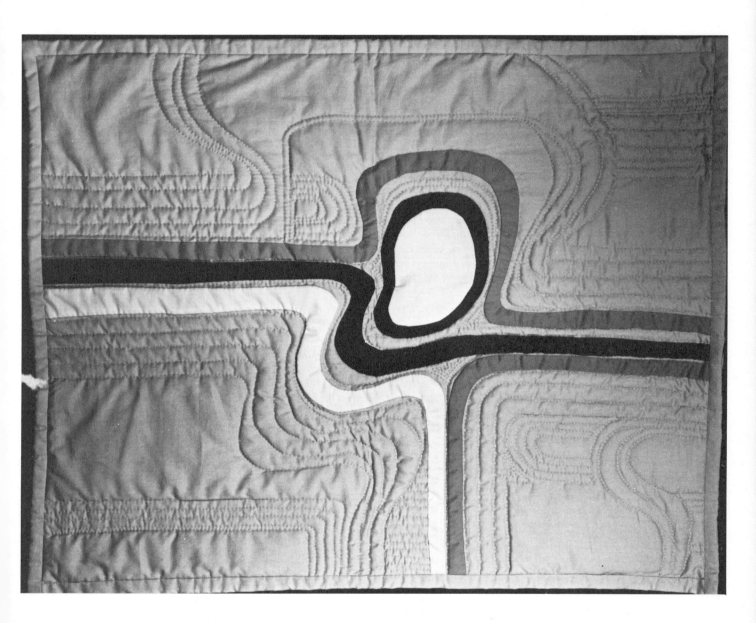

Quilted hanging, DeLoris Stude. The quilted design depicts the path of a freeway interchange, with quilting lines indicating housing, orchards, and meandering roadways.

road map. Just as the map will lead you to a destination through unfamiliar territory, strong design will lead the eye through its area to a center of interest. Following your map, you may take unexpected detours or turns, and the side trip may be full of pleasant views or interesting surprises. Or, you may find the way unmarked and be so confused that you turn back, as in a design that breaks down or is not strong enough to pull the eye along. If there is no focal point or center of interest to be the goal, the eye may be led off the edge of the design,

like a map that leads you to a bridge that has been washed out.

Components of design can be separated into elements and principles. Elements are the physical properties that you see, and principles are the way in which these properties are arranged. If the elements of a design—color, value, line, texture, and space—do not have order, then the piece becomes confusing. Design is arrangement. It is the arranging of each of the elements in an order that leads the eye through the design, sometimes with pleasant detours, but still without getting lost. Arrangement uses the principles of design—balance, rhythm, and proportion. The following sections will discuss first the elements and then the principles of design as they relate to stitchery.

Color

Visual color is seldom a flat, single color, but has reflections, highlights, and shadows, all of which make the color vary. All color is influenced by lighting and by the contrast with adjoining colors and values. For example, a red held against black will look different when held against gray or against white, and still different when held against a green. Colors vary according to hue (whether the red is red or blue), according to value (whether the red is red or pink or dark red), and according to saturation (whether the red is a bright or soft shade of the same hue).

There are four major ways of combining colors—monochromatic, analogous, complementary, and as a triad—all of which can be found using a color wheel for reference (see page 142). *Monochromatic* refers to a combination of shades and tints of the same hue but different values, such as light and dark blues.

Analogous refers to a group of colors next to each other on any segment of the wheel, such as red, yellow, and orange, or blue, blue-green, and green. These combinations may be warm, cool, or neutral. Warm colors are reds, oranges, and yellows, which are considered emotionally stimulating, and, if bright, make things appear larger or nearer. Cool colors are from the opposite side of the wheel, blues and greens, which are considered emotionally calming. In all but full intensity, they seem to recede or make things appear smaller or less apparent. Black, white, and grays are neutrals, and very muted tones such as beiges or grayed olives act as neutrals. Almost any colors can be used together without clashing if they are sufficiently neutralized, and almost any neutral works well with any bright hue.

A *complementary* color scheme uses colors opposite each other on the wheel. The complement of any color used next to it will make it appear brighter, a very useful thing to remember. Notice how many artists use small flecks, like little reflections of light, of a color's complement to give an area more light. Stitchers, too, may add tiny threads of an opposite color, or play one area against its complement to brighten the effect. Usually, a small proportion of one color to its opposite is most effective. And using a dark value of one and light value of its opposite will be more effective than colors of the same intensity. Equal areas of opposite colors of the same intensity produce a vibrating, Op-art effect, which can be garish in the wrong place. Several analogous colors can be complemented by a small amount of an opposite shade. Similarly, a dominant amount of a monochromatic color scheme can have a small amount of a bright color added for contrast.

Pegged rack holding rings of cut strands of yarn in related colors, ready to use by artist Jo Reimer.

The fourth combination is a *triad,* which is a group of colors from three equally distant points on the wheel. Again, a contrast or variation in values and proportions works best. For instance, bright purple, green, and orange would be gaudy, but a moss green and plum, both deep values, accented with a clear, light orange, could be very rich.

Value

Each color you use is light or dark, and the sum of all of them will make your total design light or dark. A strong design will have a contrast of values, using some amounts of both light and dark. If only pastel colors are used, a design will look weak, but if a deep shade of one of those colors is introduced, even sparingly, the effect will brighten. Also, if the design uses colors of all the same intensity, a flat look is achieved. Generally, designs work best with a contrast of brights and dulls.

North, a wall hanging, 7 x 14 feet, Carole Sabiston. This piece, commissioned for a London hotel, is a good example of contrasts and balance in values, lines, and textures.

Line

Design based on line, such as pencil and ink drawings, is called linear. Yet even flat contour has a line of some kind defining its shape. Stitchery is especially linear because all effects and areas are made up of the lines of yarn or thread. Lines may be straight or curved, delicate or bold, even or uneven in width. They may outline a shape, or be a part of that shape. They can suggest feeling: sharp, zig-zag, or twisting lines seem restless while gently curving or undulating lines seem calm.

Hanging, Flo Wilson. The design is built of simple lines of running stitch, woven where the lines cross. Colors are analogous violets and blue-greens on a black background.

Texture

Texture is a major component in stitchery as it relates to the texture of the total piece and of the individual yarns. Texture is perceived through our sense of touch, but experience lets us know how a surface will feel by our sight. Texture may be smooth or rough, soft or hard, fuzzy or wiry. A contrast of yarns, heavy and light, smooth and rough, adds interest to design.

Rusty gears seen through an etching screen. Experience has taught us how things feel just by what they look like. People often forget that design ideas can come from junk yards as well as nature's beauty.

Framed canvas embroidery incorporating gear parts, done in neutral colors, Judith Berni Anderson.

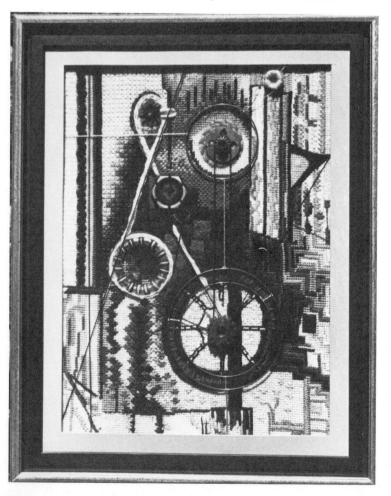

Detail of the embroidery, showing the strong textural variation resulting from the combination of metal and wool.

Space

Space effects may be actual or illusional. The physical size of the piece and the space it occupies, whether two or three dimensional, is its actual space. Illusional space is the visual perception of the piece, relating both to its actual form and to the sense of depth created within the piece by perspective, which is the artist's attempt to make a two-dimensional surface appear three dimensional. In stitchery you can achieve visual depth by arrangement of your design shapes and tonal contrast. Shapes meant to appear closer to the front should overlap shapes meant to be behind them, and should be larger with brighter, lighter, or warmer tones. Shapes meant to look far away should be smaller, and in more muted colors.

Also, in perspective, the foreground is visually sensed as the lower part, with shapes placed in the upper area appearing to be in the background, as this relates to how we see our world. Contemporary artists often ignore perspective, as primitive artists did before them, feeling that the arrangement of shapes within a given space should relate only to the actual physical area in design.

The French Fields of Grasses, Diana Bower.
Illusional space is created by a play of overlapping shapes and value contrasts.

Balance

Balance, the first of the principles of design, can be symmetrical or asymmetrical. Symmetrical balance is exactly even on each side, a formal arrangement. Asymmetrical, or informal, balance is visual, not actual. There is no formula for balance, but one can develop an awareness of it both in nature and art by observing how and where each of the design elements is placed in a composition. A small area of a bright color will balance a larger dull area. A large shape near the center of the design can be balanced by a smaller shape, farther out, just as two children of uneven weight can do on a see-saw. A small, complex area balances a larger, simple shape. It is easiest to feel balance if it is lacking. If everything looks and feels comfortable, then the design is probably balanced.

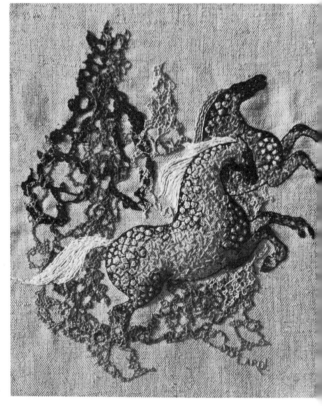

Detail of stitchery by Carol Weyhrich. Asymmetrical balance is shown in the rearing, forward motion of the horses which is held in check by the background interest.

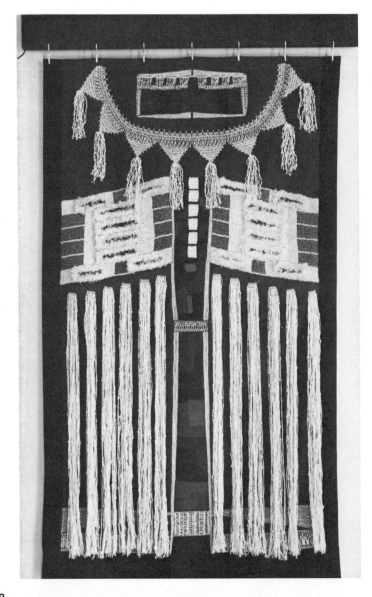

The Shaman's Coat, Flo Wilson. Symmetrical balance is created in composition on vicuna-colored coat fabric with toned suede patches for accent and stitching in white seine twine.

Rhythm

Rhythm is the way your eye moves through a design. It is often accomplished by repetition of a line, shape, or color appearing throughout the design. A checkerboard has static rhythm, in which the repetition is monotonous and does not hold your interest. Repeated units can have variety yet be strongly enough related to provide a rhythmical pattern. Negative space, or the space between design units, adds to the total rhythm, just as the pauses in music add to the effect of the melody.

Detail of stitchery by Barbara M. Day. The rhythm is achieved by the varied repetition of the figures, and the one empty figure plays strongly on the rhythm of negative space between the figures.

Proportion

The strength of a design depends on the proportions or relative size, amount, and placement of each element. The choice of the size and scale of a design in proportion to the over-all area can change a design from a small accent to a major design unit. On a garment, a design repeat might be the same figure, but worked in large scale near the bottom, getting smaller as it nears the face. A large geometric design might be alternated with multiple units of the same design on small scale.

Proportion also includes color dominance. If, in your stitchery, you use a color scheme taken from a painting, a print, or even a rug, be sure you note the proportion of each color in the original—which are dominant, which are only accents. Otherwise, the color scheme may appear different in the differing scale of your stitchery. For example, a bright blue would overwhelm a soft green if used in the same amount, but would be a pleasing accent if used in a small amount.

DESIGN BY ARRANGEMENT

Unity or harmony is achieved when all of these things work smoothly together. Variety within unity adds strength. A better measure of an artist than drawing skill is achieving good design, and the best way to learn how to design is just experimenting. Work for the pleasure of what you are doing, with the end product secondary for a while. There are many ways of designing that involve no drawing or "art" skills. If you are concerned about reproducing objects realistically, ask yourself what is "real" in art. A traditionally reproduced grouping of apples on a plate might look real enough but may or may not be good design. Do you like it because it is familiar, and there is no need to look at it objectively? A nostalgic farm scene can bring back fond memories; therefore you judge it good according to subjective memories- rather than with any appreciation of what the artist has or has not accomplished. Don't confuse realistic with familiar. Microscopic cellular patterns, cross-section slices of vegetables, and a tree trunk through a magnifying glass are all very real; yet they could be rendered true to form without being recognized because they appear so abstract. Design can be a microscopic or a magnified view of an ordinary item or shapes so simplified from nature as to lose identity. They are still, perhaps, very realistic, just unfamiliar.

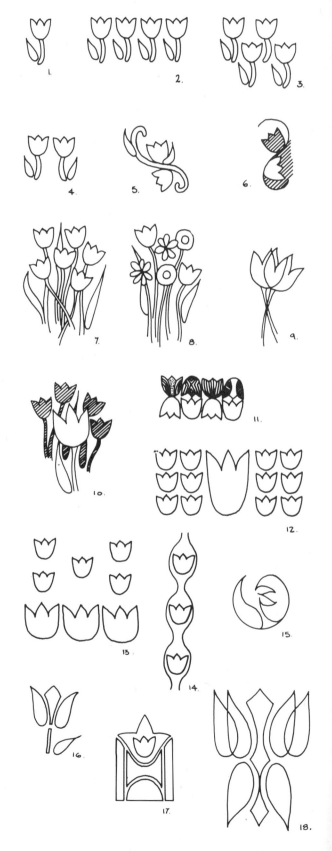

Drawing made after a notebook page done by Ann Spiess Mills. Mrs. Mills' figures show an ability to represent objects recognizably and stylistically.

RED - FACE APPLIQUÉ TO RED GINGHAM HOOD THIS TO HOPSACKING THE REST IS EMBROIDERY.

FOR CAPE - USE RED HOPSACKING, RED AND WHITE GINGHAM LINING. FROGS CAN BE COVERED BUTTONS WITH EMBROIDERY. A LADYBUG ON THE BACK!

PUT IN PLENTY OF HEM. SHOULD BE WORN A COUPLE OF YEARS.

A BASKET WITH DRAW-STRING FABRIC FOR PURSE. LINE IT WITH PLASTIC TO CARRY LUNCH.

WOLF - USE CALICO PRINT FOR JACKET - PLAID FOR PANTS. APPLIQUE TO HOPSACKING - EMBROIDER THE REST.

GRANNY'S SHAWL IS STILL ANOTHER CALICO PIECE. HER FACE IS APPLIQUED, THE REST EMBROIDERY. USE HOOK AND EYE - EYE FOR GLASSES.

Opposite:
Design variations from one shape: (1) simplified tulip shape, (2) repeating in even row, (3) staggered repeat, (4) mirror reverse, (5) rearrangement of design elements along a curved line, (6) counter-change of positive and negative areas of tulip head, (7) random combination with changed stem scale, (8) combination with related shapes, (9) offset units, (10) overlapped units varying in scale, (11) repeated pattern with filling variations, (12) repeated pattern with scale variation, (13) repeated pattern for border with scale variations, (14) repeated pattern enclosed in related shape, (15) design elements distorted to fit a predetermining space, (16) dissected design elements, (17, 18) rearrangements of the dissected shapes to form new or abstract designs.

Pictures on the following pages:

1
Color wheel showing each yarn color worked out in four textures, Maggie Turner. Photograph by Jacqueline Enthoven.

2
Dyed hanks of yarn placed in the sequence of colors on a color wheel.

3
Analogous colors in warm tones with an accent of blue and green.

4
Analogous colors in cool tones with an accent of yellow, a complementary color from the other side of the color wheel.

5
Yarns of varying textures, dyed in neutral tones by Flo Wilson. The four yarn schemes were dyed and photographed by Flo Wilson.

6
The stitchery of Ann Speiss Mills is a colorful folk art. Padded cross, showing San Pasqual, the patron saint of cooking in New Mexico and Mexico, is typical of her work.

7
Angel with mandolin, courtesy of Mrs. Benny Ross. Angels are about 17 inches tall. Body, head, dress, and sleeves are cut out together with matching piece for back. Arms, and mandolin, are made separately, stuffed, and inserted in sleeves.

8
Pixie boot, given as a gift full of pecans and later filled with greens for the holiday. It is made of three pieces of felt—front, back, and sole.

9
Angel of peace, holding the lion and lamb, collection of the author. Curls on animals and angel are French knots. The skirts of angels are left open at bottom so they can sit atop a Christmas tree.

10
Hearts used for Christmas ornaments, collection of the author. As in all Mrs. Mills' work, pieces are joined by buttonhole-stitches.

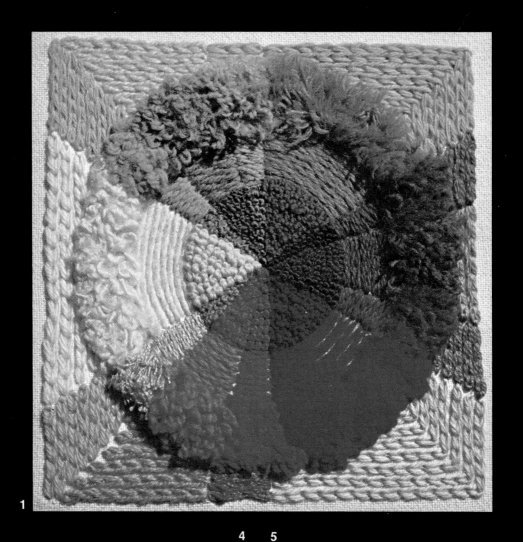

1

2 3 4 5

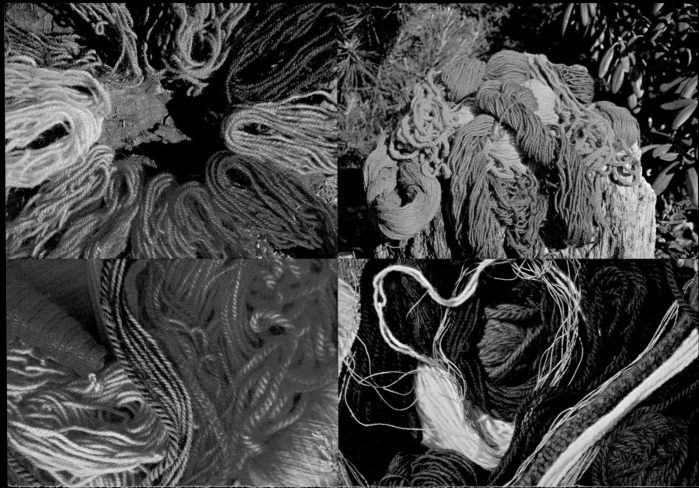

a

b

True abstraction is achieved when the artist can use his knowledge of elements and principles of design, and arrange things just for the sheer joy of making pleasing or interesting shapes, textures, and lines that "belong" together. When a design is successful it is because it has become something pleasing of itself, not because it looks like something else that is pleasing.

Design is much easier if it is considered as arrangement. Architects arrange spaces for buildings, stage designers arrange furniture for actors to move through, homemakers arrange flowers or table settings, we all arrange our daily outfits—blending colors of shirts and suits, adding a center of interest with a scarf, tie, or pin. The difference, and difficulty, is that an artist designs with shapes that are not yet there. So, to make your designing easier, build a series of shapes first, whether cut from paper or magazines, or made of folded paper and collected objects. Then arrange them on a surface—and you have created a design.

Three depictions of animals that are recognizable enough to be called realistic, but varied enough to show individual styles of the artists: (a) leopard by Carol Weyhrich, (b) elephant by Irene Ohashi, (c) burro by Ann Spiess Mills.

c

Distance is a powerful abstractor. This is a real view of meandering lines following land contours, taken from an airplane.

Mechanical or physical aids are useful in many areas of design. A simple tool to help make you become more aware of patterns in nature is a view finder (see drawing). Cut a rectangle approximately 3 x 5 inches out of a larger piece of cardboard, leaving a wide border. Or cut two right angles that can be manipulated to form rectangles of various sizes.

Then, using this view finder, go through magazines with large-size pictures. Slide your view finder in various angles until the part in the viewer is pleasing to you. Avoid a complete scene; instead, look for parts of the whole which form pleasing shapes or colors without identification of subject matter. Mark the view and cut it out. Collect at least 25 of these designs, all of the same size. Go through the list of design elements and principles and see if you can find a few examples of each in your collection, and several color combinations. Match each shade and color of your favorite example with small lengths of yarn. Twist the strands together and knot to keep as a reminder of a color scheme you like. Finally, lay several of your cut shapes on a flat surface and see if you can arrange them into a larger, pleasing combination.

Random arrangement of rectangles found in a picture of lumber ends.

An ordered arrangement of rectangles with strong value contrasts, found in a lumber yard.

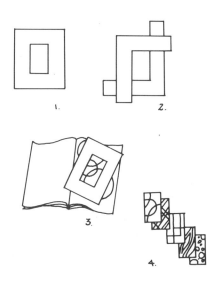

Using a viewfinder: (1) cut a frame, or (2) a pair of right angles to form an adjustable frame, (3) use frame on a magazine with large illustrations to find interesting patterns within them, and (4) cut out a series of these views to study them separately and in various combinations.

An arrangement of even repeats of varied rectangles with projections indicating illusional space, found in a picture of cut lumber ends.

There are many ways to build a design by arrangement. A trip to the dimestore will provide several inexpensive tools to aid simple drawing, such as colored felt-tipped pens, a ruler, a tablet of tracing paper, graph paper, a plastic right angle, and a plastic French curve. A pair of scissors and a supply of cheap paper such as newsprint are handy aids for manipulating shapes. Pens and tailor's chalk will help when working directly on fabric.

Now, cut freehand from newsprint a series of about 15 rectangles of various proportions. The edges may be slightly rounded, or the shapes a little modified if you prefer. Choosing from your pile of shapes, manipulate them on a piece of fabric until you like the arangement. Pin them to the fabric, and mark around each with tailor's chalk or

A French-curve shape available in plastic, and two designs derived from it below. The designs are created by laying the curve at various angles, and choosing which curves to join.

basting thread, forming the outlines for your sampler. Where shapes overlap, consider which shape is to be seen as closer, and plan to use a different shade of thread in the overlapping area, to indicate transparency. Using one of the color schemes suggested by your exeperiment with the view finder, fill in each of the areas with stitchery.

Cut-paper shapes can involve folding paper in halves, fourths, or eighths, and cutting into the edges as you did when you were a child making paper snowflakes or strings of paper dolls. Cut any shape and repeat the units, identically or with minor variations, along evenly spaced areas according to a line or grid, or along a flowing uneven pattern. To create a grid for spacing, fold a large piece of newsprint four or five times both crosswise and lengthwise. Unfold and you have a sheet divided into many sections to use as a basis for spacing. The arrangement might be closer in one area, farther apart in another, which would make use of the rhythmic variations in negative space. Arrangement of design shapes can also be done with string, cut straws, toothpicks, seeds, or buttons. Anything that can represent shapes, lines, or textures can be planned visually and then transferred to fabric to form the outline of a stitchery.

Here is a checklist of design experiments:
(1) Use a view finder to see new shapes and patterns.
(2) Vary the order of a repeat, in a line, stair-step, or grid pattern.
(3) Vary the positive and negative part of a design. Counterchange is the name for a variation using both the shape cut out and the background negative area.
(4) Repeat a design in mirror reverse.
(5) Enclose your shape in a surrounding shape or block.
(6) Use your shape as a part of a larger shape.
(7) Offset, or slightly overlap, one shape and its repeat.
(8) Using your shape as a center, build a design outward from it. Or using your shape as the outside contour, divide the inside space into design areas.

Orange Sections, Jo Reimer. This stitchery is based on an abstract series of shapes, which have been "exploded" to suggest separating orange segments.

Birdheads, Jean Wilson. The head shapes have been adapted to fill the spaces, so that each fits together.

EXPERIMENTING WITH FABRICS

Looking at a printed fabric with eyes that see it as a collection of color and pattern areas to build into new compositions will add many ideas to your designs for stitchery. Usually in stitchery one adds pattern to a plain fabric, but it can be stimulating to use fabric that already has a pattern printed on it. The artist may also print a plain fabric and then embellish it with stitchery, as in various silkscreen processes or tie-dyeing and tie-bleaching. Within limits, fabric can also be painted and stitched.

In planning your design, consider the print as an abstract breakup of space rather than a representation of subject matter. The fabric itself may suggest what might be done with it, such as cutting out various shapes and using them as appliqués on another part of the fabric, or leaving them where they were printed, but adding padding. Also you might make a large-scale appliqué shape, of a flower for example, that uses several prints together —perhaps each petal can be a different print. The scales of the prints must be similar and the color schemes harmonious for this to work. Adding texture to the applied print and carrying lines out into the surrounding stitchery is a technique that works well in modifying ready-made clothes (see Chapter 2). You might decorate various portions of the existing pattern with stitchery, without rearranging anything. Surface embroidery, quilting, and trapunto all lend themselves to these accents. Since variety within unity is one of the embracing principles of design, consider your added stitches as variations on the print itself, with an eye toward strengthening the total, rather than merely filling in the lines or shapes, with texture and color.

Stitchery added to a prized print from Fortuny, by the author. This print has special memories attached to it, as it was bought as a result of a visit to the owner of the firm, Countess Elsie Lee Gozzi, at Giudecca, Venice, where the showrooms and factory are. Courtesy A. T. Norman.

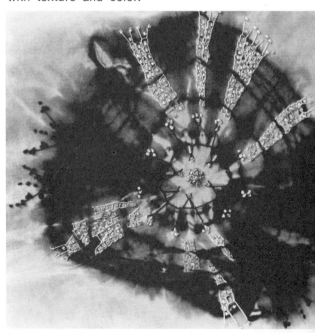

Detail of skirt, Barbara Meier. *Special Methods:* the navy velveteen cloth was tie-bleached, then dyed to a muted pink and embellished with stitchery and beads.

Detail of skirt, Ann Spiess Mills. *Special Methods:* acrylic paint was applied with a dry brush on a polyester knit, and highlighted with stitchery. If the fabric becomes too thick with paint it is difficult to stitch through. *Variation:* the painted polyester is washable with care, but better results are had on cotton, where the colors remain more vivid after washing.

Detail of vest, Linda Batway. An entire pattern repeat has been completely outlined in several rows of stem stitch, which follow and reinforce the print, and hide it entirely.

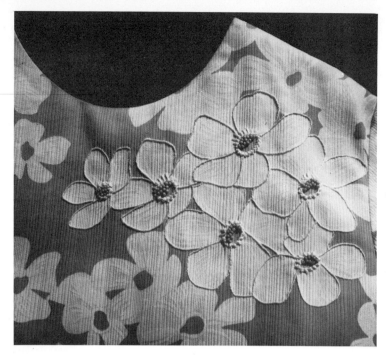

Detail of stitchery on floral pattern, Jacqueline Enthoven. Photograph by Jacqueline Enthoven. The even print has been given a designer's touch with stem-stitch, knots, and beads.

Detail of stitchery incorporating a print as part of a larger, new design, Jill Nordfors.

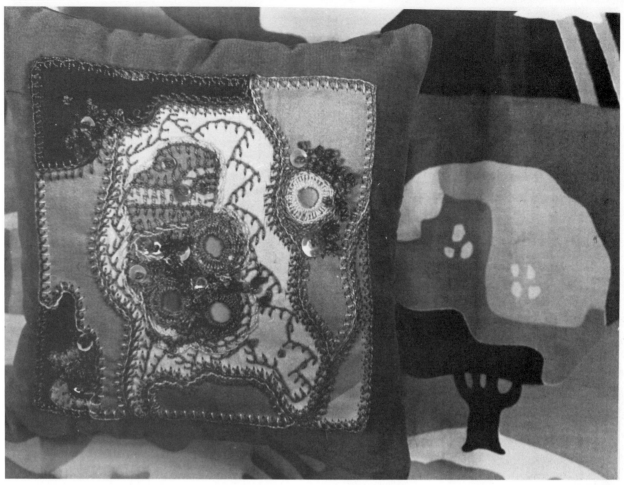

Pincushions using prints as abstract areas of color to build entirely new designs, Mary Ann Spawn. Each cushion sits on a background of the fabric used in its construction, in which the scale of the design is much larger than the scale of the final object (6 x 6 inches) so that the new patterns bear little relationship to the original printed pattern.

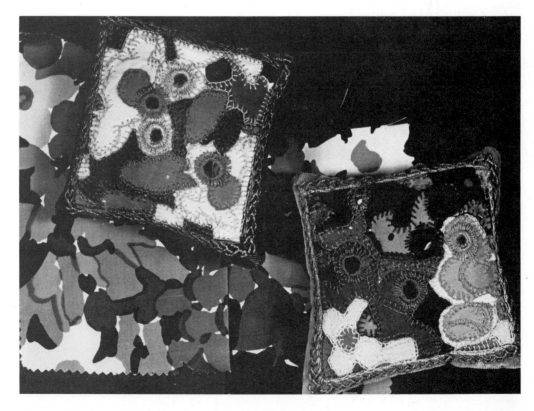

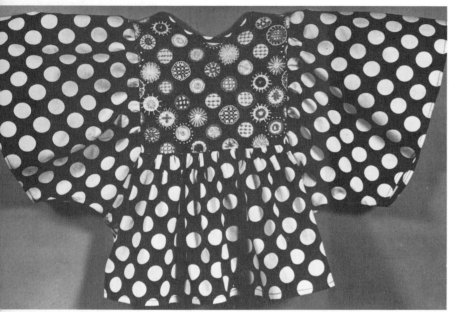

Polka-dot blouse, with embellished dots, Pat
Albiston. Details show stitchery on dots and
back-yoke buttons.

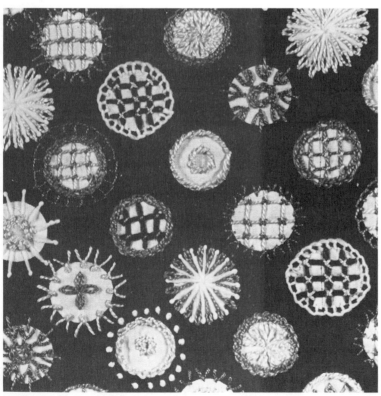

Of course prints come in a wide variety of sizes, shapes, and placement of patterns. Over-all patterns may be tiny or huge, overlapping or widely spaced, and range from definite, contained shapes to flowing colors that are completely abstracted. If the pattern is evenly spaced you might want to embellish parts of it. If it is widely spaced, you might build new shapes between, such as adding vines or a trellis pattern to a floral print. Stripes can be filled with rows of stitches to make them more delicate in appearance, or strengthened with bold stitches. Very interesting color effects can be achieved by stripes of different or matching colors.

At times, a totally new pattern can be achieved by cutting and rearranging the stripes in new patterns. A stripe might be cut into strips of random width, arranged at right angles to the other stripes and then shifted up or down, or various sections turned in different directions. If the stripes are figured, try turning one of the sections so that it

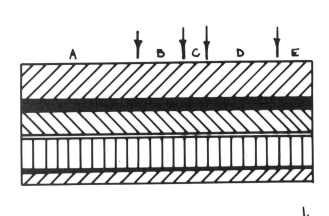

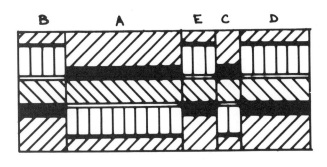

Rearranging a striped fabric: a length of evenly striped fabric is cut across at the arrows, then pieces are rearranged as shown to form a new pattern. Quilting or stitchery might be added to the new arrangement, or it could be used as the basis for a different design in stitchery.

Rearranged pattern cut from two batiked silk patterns, one checked and one irregularly striped, Katherine Gorham. Photo by Katherine Gorham. The resulting design was padded and stitched for added dimension.

runs up instead of down. After you have found a pleasing arrangement, sew the stripes together in their new position, and press. This will show you an entirely new break-up of space, which you might embellish with stitchery or use as a model for a new design of your own. Other patterns besides stripes can be cut and reassembled, but the design factors become increasingly complex, and you might try the experiment first with stripes.

Striped pattern rearranged and stitched to form abstracted initials, Mary Hanson, courtesy of Jean Wilson.

Striped pincushion, Mary Ann Spawn. The fabric, shown in the background, was applied to velveteen and stitched in such a way that the original pattern no longer appears to be a figured stripe.

5 LEARNING AND JUDGING STITCHERY

In years past, needlework was a skill taught by one generation to the next. Women took pride in developing their skill in adding beauty to handmade clothing and household articles, and in teaching that skill to their daughters. When the hand skills were no longer necessary, many women continued their needlework for pleasure, but the family no longer depended on their activity, and the chain of learning was broken.

LEARNING STITCHERY
Now we must go to classes or to books and magazines to find what was once taught in the family. The stitcher must sift through a wealth of instructions trying to find those that have the most merit.

Love Quilt, a gift to stitchery teacher and author, Jacqueline Enthoven by Northwest artists. Participating artists, *from top, left to right:* Maylie Donaldson, Edith Carlson, Flo Wilson, Susan Roach, Jean Wilson, Jill Nordfors, Fritzi Oxley, Pat Albiston, Beverly Rush, Lassie Wittman, Mary Ann Spawn, Jo Reimer, Maggie Turner, Patty Price, Betty Jensen.

In general, the printed instructions are of two sorts —those that teach only the stitches and those that try to encourage creativity and good design, such as Jacqueline Enthoven's *The Stitches of Creative Embroidery,* rather than just copying from the instructions. A teacher in a class can provide a third element: feedback and evaluation of what the student is doing. This support is invaluable in the constructive development of a sense of design. Interestingly, even the teachers of stitchery indicate they often feel insecure in teaching design, and might welcome a review of the design elements and principles discussed in the previous chapter, as well as the objective standards for evaluation of work that will be discussed in this chapter.

Students in stitchery classes generally fall into two categories. First there are those who have started with an interest in embroidery, but find that working someone else's design is not enough, and they hope to learn to create their own work. Then there are students who have an interest in art, and see stitchery as a new means of creative expression. Each group can spark the other, and the most stimulating classes are likely to have students of both types.

Student and teacher will soon become involved in judging the quality of work being done. But how should a stitchery be judged? Royalty of old prized only the rarest and costliest of materials and threads, the most highly skilled hands, and cartoons (drawn designs) created by famous artists. Today we are much more appreciative of the fact that good art can be everywhere, produced from even the most common materials and discards or found objects. The hand-dyed, handspun, and handwoven appeal to us, perhaps because machines are so good at imitating anything which is highly precise. The arts of the primitive cultures seem rare and valuable today, and so we add fur, bones, quills, and shells to our textiles.

All evaluation comes down to three elements: quality of design, interest of materials, and quality of craftsmanship. It is possible to do very fine work on poor materials—for instance burlap, which will fade in color and deteriorate after a few years. It is also possible to do very sloppy work within the outline of a good design, so that the closer you come to a piece the worse it looks! There is a vast difference, however, between sloppy work and careful work that has a free spontaneous quality (although neither would satisfy a lover of precise details). Quickly done pieces meant to last only a short time also have their place, but if you are putting much time and effort into a stitchery, you will probably want to use fabric and yarns of good quality.

Free-form stitchery applied to driftwood, by the author, courtesy of Audree Rush. Contemporary standards value common materials and found objects more highly than in the past.

Length of handwoven fabric with stitchery incorporating driftwood and hung from pieces of driftwood, by the author. Since machines can so easily create textiles, handmade fabric has new value in modern times.

Two Danish fishing hoops, with organically arranged flow of fibers including fur and horsehair, and leather and beads, by Helen J. Rumpel. Materials used functionally by primitive cultures—such as fur and horsehair—now add decorative interest to a stitchery because they are rarely seen in works of art.

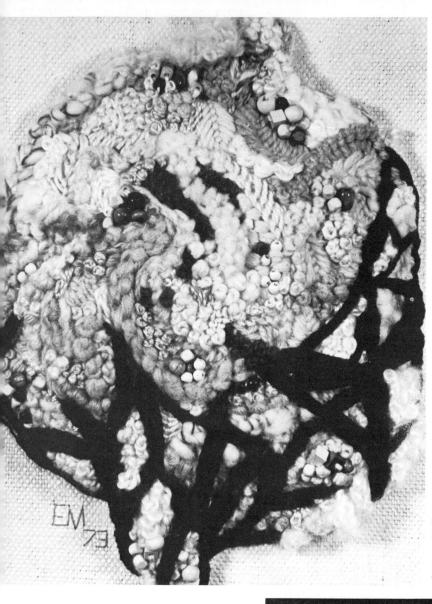

Shells and seed pods capture our imaginations by reminding us of the world of nature hidden in our industrial age. *Seed Pod,* heavily textured and padded, Elsa Mann; padded and shaded shell, Janet Wetzig Collins.

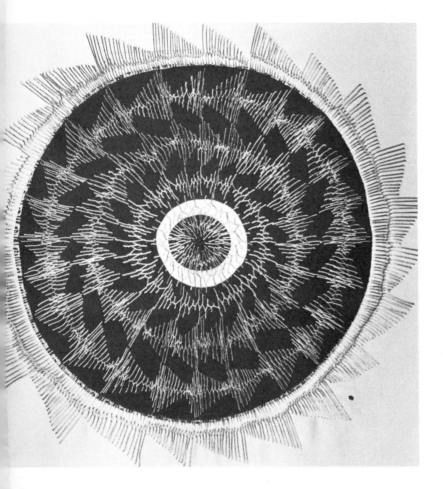

The best teaching always involves evaluation, although on a more informal level than that done by a jury for a show or exhibit. By keeping the discussion to a consideration of design properties, use of materials, and craftsmanship, rather than emotional reactions, which are inevitably subjective, the whole class can participate in the evaluation and learn from one another. Some of the following questions may help such a discussion get started.

(1) Are the materials and stitches appropriate to the design and function of the piece?
(2) Does it show an expressive or imaginative use of materials and stitches?
(3) Does it show a good use of space, with a variety of sizes, lengths, and direction of positive and negative shapes?
(4) Is the scale of the design appropriate to the total scale and to each part of the design?
(5) Is there a center of interest, and does the eye move rhythmically through the design? Is there a feeling of balance?
(6) Is there a good contrast of colors and value in the design?
(7) Does the design unify the various elements such as lines, shapes, colors, contrasts, and texture?
(8) Finally, have the special variations and effects that stitchery offers been used to full advantage, rather than forcing the design to imitate another medium?

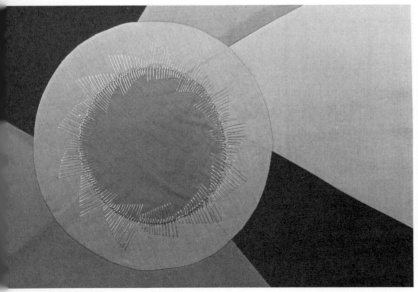

Three banners worked from a class assignment, by Maylie Donaldson in a class taught by Katherine Gorham. Using a commercial print as a base, the design was embellished, modified, or disguised.

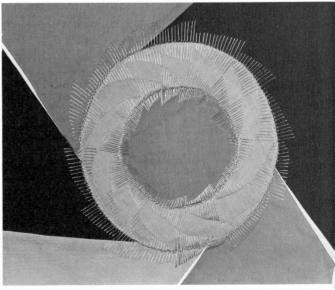

Then a new design was created by combining elements from the first two stitcheries to create a third. Here the elements transferred were stitches and shapes.

Russian Landscape, Diana Bower. Print fabric has been used as a pattern of fields around an icy pond and to create summer palaces now used as granaries. The effect of appliqué and decorative stitches transforms a painterly design into something that has the special charm of stitchery.

Hanging panel, Kathy Cole. In this ingenious use of stitchery, made on separately mounted units, the design advances and recedes, giving the effect of shadow and depth. The tree branches, the grass, and the shingles on the house have been treated simply but effectively with long stitches. The flat areas of the house and some tree shapes were silk-screened by the artist, to form a variation of background.

Stitchery of home-canned jar of vegetables, Lassie Wittman. What kind of exhibit would be appropriate for this piece?

SHOWS AND EXHIBITS

The stitcher who has always considered embroidery a personal craft will find herself in a whole new world when she takes a stitchery class based on design. Not only will it open her eyes to the world around her, but she will start hearing references to exhibits, shows, galleries, and jurying—all signs that stitchery has been accepted in the world of art. How are pieces chosen for these shows and who chooses them? If you become part of a group sponsoring a show that includes stitchery, as many needlecraft guilds and groups do, you may find yourself called upon to sit on the other side of the fence, and to judge which pieces are acceptable. How are you going to choose, and how are you going to ensure that the show is a constructive experience for those entering?

The purpose of shows or exhibits is to provide exposure for artists and sometimes outlets for sales. Awards are given as a way of building the artist's reputation. By attending several stitchery exhibits you will begin to see that the works accepted for one may be very different from those accepted for another. This does not add up to the too-frequent conclusion that there is no basis for opinion in art; it only means that there is room for wide variation and human interpretation of design. Just as one artist is more interested in one aspect of art than in others, so are those who select work for shows (jurying) and award prizes (judging). Some shows include stitchery along with other art media, which means that the piece is judged strictly on its merits as art. Some shows, frequently those connected with university galleries, are more interested in pieces that explore new frontiers, that experiment with new uses of materials and new ways to use them. On the other hand, an exhibit connected with an historical museum would be inclined to show more interest in a knowledge of the way the skill was traditionally practiced. Your county fair will probably be interested in reflecting the kind of skills found in traditional homes. The point is, if you feel inclined to show your work for the first time, consider where the most appropriate outlet is *for you*. A rejection may mean simply that the piece was entered in the wrong show.

JURYING AND JUDGING

Recently, the Columbia Stitcher's Guild in Portland, Oregon held a workshop to evolve guidelines for shows sponsored by their guild, in order that maximum understanding and growth could be achieved. Their system of evaluation, while meant for a group show, has much merit for a teacher with her class or even for self-evaluation.

The question of whether or not non-members should be included in the show must be decided before anything else, and can be viewed from several angles. A guild show usually represents many kinds of stitchers whereas a gallery might want to limit its entrants to a special sort of artist. On the other hand, a group benefits by widening its horizon and extending an invitation to the many artists who are not joiners by nature. The show may be an incentive for such an artist to share interests with members (perhaps even to join). Or, a group may want to limit the show to its members, who probably already share certain standards and interests, to keep the atmosphere more informal and provide a sociable learning experience for those who already know one another.

Each piece must be an original design. Kits, copies of kits, or custom designs should never be judged in the same show with the original designs, unless there is a separate category for such work, clearly marked as such.

Three classes of entries are accepted, based on the artist's own choice of class: beginner, intermediate, and advanced. This refers to the work, not the artist, since an advanced artist in canvaswork may be a beginner in surface stitchery, and so on.

All pieces are juried according to a known point system, and the number of points determines whether the piece is hung. There is also an unjuried section of the same show, where each member may have one piece. This system has several commendable aspects. The entrant chooses her own level of competition. An outlet is provided for those who do not wish to compete. Comments by the jurors and the point breakdown, which is based on a known system, give the entrant a tangible, constructive evaluation of her work.

There are several jurors, chosen by the Exhibit Committee, usually from teachers or outstanding artists in the area. A subtractive point system was found more workable than an additive one. Each entry starts with a total of 100 points, divided as follows: design and composition, 25; color usage, 20; suitability of materials, 10; craftsmanship, including the appropriate use of stitches, 30; and finishing or framing, 15. Points are then subtracted for weak areas. In addition, each juror may award a limited number of merit awards based on overall impact, not points. This evaluation, including points awarded, is returned with the entry on a juror's scorecard with space for added comments. Each entrant thus knows what the strong or weak points of her piece were considered to be.

Ladybug, by Jacqueline Enthoven, added for personality to a ready-made blouse.

VARYING YOUR VOCABULARY OF STITCHES

If you are interested in stitchery, you must have found several sources of different stitches by now, and worked a sampler or two. This section is concerned not with teaching basic stitches, but with showing you how to vary those you already know or will acquire.

Stitches may be used in one of several ways. Many very effective designs use only the simplest of stitches, with minor or no variations from the traditional method taught. After several pieces, however, many stitchers feel a great urge to learn more. While knowing a vast number of stitches is a challenge, it is the artist who explores the possibility within each stitch that has the greatest "vocabulary" of stitches, even though the number may not be so impressive. This exploration can actually be combined within a finished piece by limiting yourself to using only one stitch for an entire design and varying that stitch until the space is filled.

A good way to become thoroughly familiar with a stitch is to take a piece of fabric of relatively loose, even weave, such as burlap or monk's cloth. Try the same stitch in as many ways as you can think of. Not all stitches will be successful in all variations—but try it anyway, and you might invent something new.

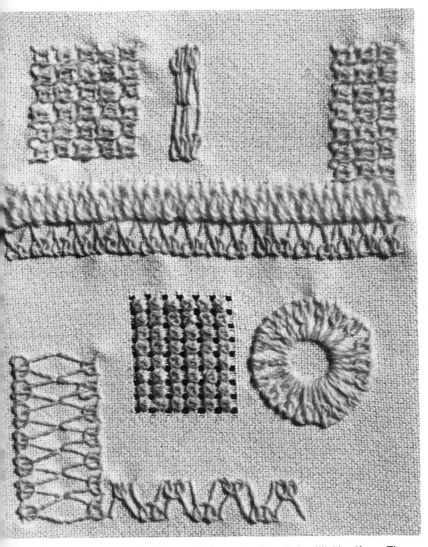

Variations of the sorbello-stitch, Jill Nordfors. The stitches are used in even geometric rows in many of these variations.

Variations of the Vandyke-stitch, by the author. The stitches are used as free-moving lines to establish a pattern.

The simplest way to use a stitch is in even or geometric repeats, as in needlepoint stitches and cross-stitch. These even rows are then built up to make designs. The second way to use stitches is in free-moving lines used to outline or establish a pattern. Simple or intricate, the pattern is more apparent than the stitch used, which blends into the design. The third way to use a stitch is as a texture, where the varying rhythm of the stitch itself becomes the design. Here, a pattern may not be recognizable. It is the texture of the yarn and stitches that are important.

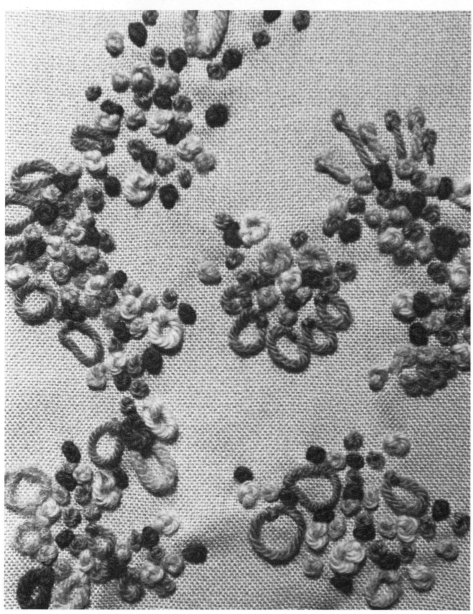

Design with Chinese knot, Flo Wilson. The stitches establish a pattern here, too.

Detail of *Shaman's Coat,* Flo Wilson, using Turkey-work, the Palestrina knot, and seeding to create texture.

When you experiment with a stitch, first try the stitch in the conventional way, with a thread that will easily define the structure of the stitch, such as perle cotton. Next, vary the kinds of yarn: thick, thin, lumpy, fuzzy, wiry, and so forth. The stitch structure will almost disappear if the yarn is fuzzy enough.

Next, distort the stitch shape by elongating, shortening, bending, or making zig-zags. Alternate the treatment of the stitch in a single area, first orderly and tight, then in a loose, relaxed variation.

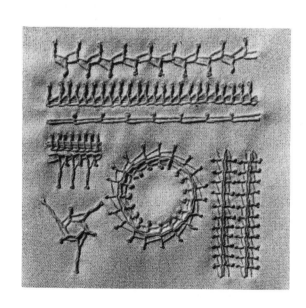

Variations of the Vandyke-stitch, Flo Wilson. The yarn is varied and produces very different effects. The thin, light yarn is threaded through the thicker stitches.

Variations of the crested chain-stitch, Jill Nordfors. Note that the parts of the stitch have been distorted—some made longer, some smaller—to produce very dissimilar rows. Variations on circles are also shown.

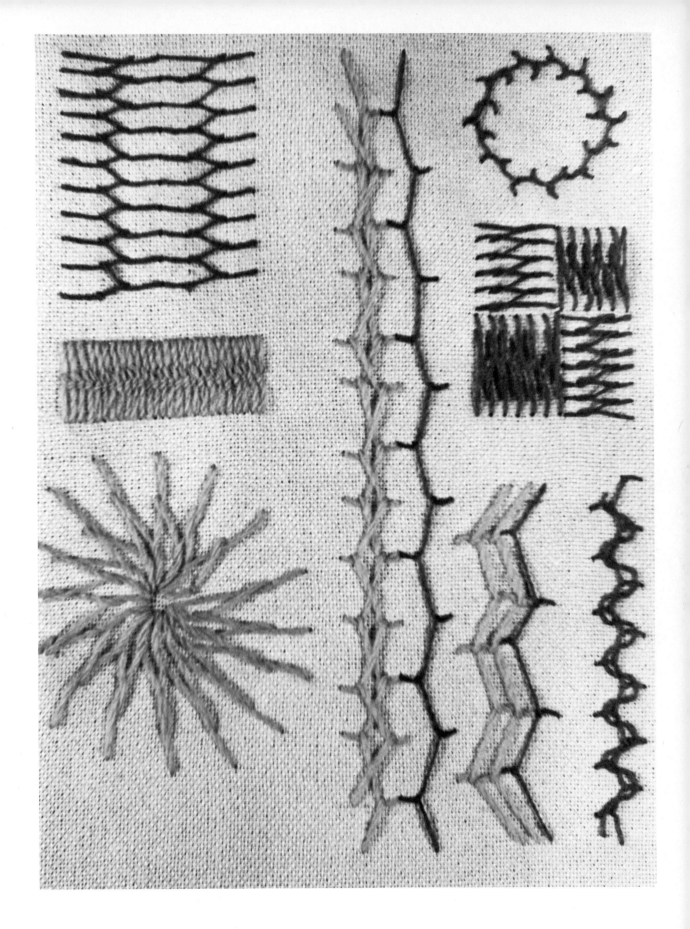

Variations of Cretan-stitch, Jill Nordfors. Here the variation is mostly in the expansion of the stitch—wide apart at top left, close together beneath that. The effect of zig-zags are shown at bottom right.

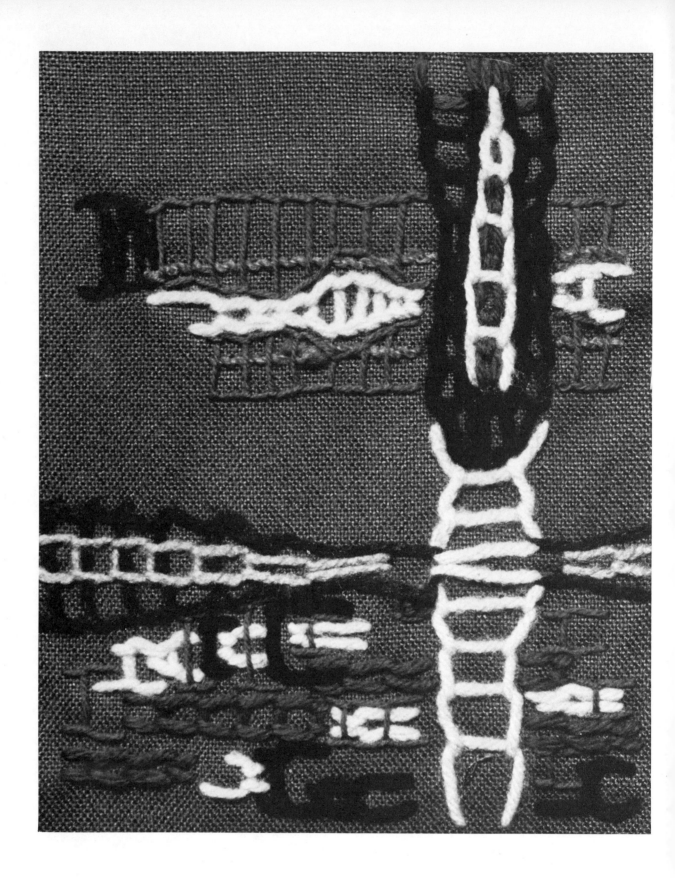

Try combining the stitch in rows: two or more touching rows, overlapping rows, back-to-back or dovetailed rows. Make blocks of these rows, using the stitches both open and closely spaced. Stitch one row on top of another while varying color, yarn, or both. Make two more rows, whipping a second thread through the stitches of one (always from the same direction) and threading a second thread back and forth through the stitches of the other.

Variations of the squared chain-stitch, Flo Wilson. The interesting patterns that can be made with linking and overlapping rows have been explored.

Relate the rows in various ways by combining with similar or different stitches, adding knots, or stitching in circular patterns. Fan stitches out from the center, as the spokes on a wheel. Run a line of stitches in a circle as a rim. Try using the stitch as an edging, attached on one side only to a folded edge of fabric. Try a second row, attached to the loose edge, making a detached stitch.

Variations of the crested chain-stitch, Flo Wilson. Even and loose stitches in geometric rows are varied by color.

Variations of the sorbello-stitch, Flo Wilson. The varying relation between rows of color and placement of rows forms an interesting abstract all made from a single stitch.

Couching stitch explored while creating a horse-like figure, Flo Wilson. Note the interesting use of couched-on loops for the mane.

Necklace detail, Flo Wilson. Beads are attached with a regular stitch of a Palestrina knot.

Use the stitch as couching, that is over another yarn that lies on the surface, varying heavy yarn over lighter, lighter over heavier. Instead of couching to a fabric, try working the stitch over a detached sturdy cord. Try attaching a second row of covered cord to the first with stitches working into the first row. Finally, attach beads with the stitch, in a regular pass of the thread in the stitch, or around or on top of the stitch.

The variations and combinations of stitches can be almost endless, but these ideas should provide you with a checklist of some of them, and you can work your own after you get started. Use a notebook-sized piece of fabric for your sampler. You can keep the "pages" in a three-ring binder for reference after making holes at the edge.

Variations of using beads with stitchery, Susan Roach.

GLOSSARY AND INDEX TO TECHNIQUES

This cross-referenced list will help you find techniques, and some materials and articles, that are scattered throughout the text and captions. All of them should be considered for possible use on projects—there are no set rules. Definitions are geared more to practical use than historically accurate terminology, which has often led to several different names for the same technique. Very familiar terms have not been defined. Where additional information can be found in another listing in the Glossary, the word indicating that entry will be CAPITALIZED.

Italian quilting, two narrow parallel lines for a linear design stitched through two layers. Yarn is then entered from the lining side and run through the design, forming a raised ridge between the two lines. The width of the parallel lines depends on, or determines, the thickness of the yarn to be used, 22

trapunto, quilting of design area in an otherwise unpadded surface. In one method, the design is outlined by stitching through only the top layer and lining, and padding is inserted afterwards by slashing the lining (which should be a FABRIC that does not ravel easily), stuffing, and resewing the lining with whip STITCHES. In another method, the design is stitched through all three layers and then the excess padding is cut away, 22, 46, 82, 83, 148

quilts, see BEDCOVERS

reverse appliqué, see APPLIQUÉ

room dividers, 10, 15, 18, 19, 22, 23, 25, also see MOUNTING TECHNIQUES

samplers, STITCHERY done for practice, often a combination of many stitches in a decorative panel, 15, 20, 146, 163, 171

screen construction, see MOUNTING TECHNIQUES

seat covers, see UPHOLSTERY and CANVASWORK

seeding, an EMBROIDERY technique in which small STITCHES, knots, or BEADING is scattered over a large area to create texture or pattern

sewed construction:
    collars, 96
    dolls, 38
    handbags, 112, 113, 114, 116, 118, 122, 123–124, also see FABRIC, GUSSETS, INTERFACING, PATTERN DRAFTING, and PATCHWORK

shaped stitchery, see SOFT SCULPTURE

shaped weaving, WEAVING in which selvages are not parallel but angled or curved. Can be created on a warp stretched over nails or pegs on a frame or board. Where area is small and warp is close together, the filling is drawn through with a needle, relating this to NEEDLEWEAVING. Since the nails can be placed in specific patterns, this technique can be used to create woven clothing and accessories to shape, 87, 89

shi-sha, see ATTACHMENT

shows, see EXHIBITING

soft sculpture, three-dimensional shapes of STITCHERY, MACRAMÉ, WRAPPING, etc. If, instead of using STUFFING or an armature, the stitchery covers a hard object such as a cube or box, it might better be called "fiber sculpture," 32, 33, 45, 48, also see MOUNTING TECHNIQUES

sportsclothes, 77, 78, 79

stitchery, a term currently applied to needlework and handstitching of all kinds, including EMBROIDERY, CANVASWORK, CREWELWORK, NEEDLE LACE, and NEEDLEWEAVING. Frequently stitchers include also APPLIQUÉ, PATCHWORK, and QUILTING in their work. Stitchery implies a freer approach to needlework, in which the old boundaries are broken down and many techniques are combined, 10, 13, 15, 16, 17, 18, 20, 32, 50, 51, 54, 73, 78, 90, 96, 104, 108, 112, 113, 126, 138, 139, 141, 146, 148, 149, 150, 152, 156, 158, 159, 162

stitches mentioned: Bayeaux, 73; blanket, 131; blind, 13, 20, 32, 38, 53, 81, 96, 104, 113, 116, 118; Bokhara, 15; buttonhole, 23, 24, 32, 41, 56, 74, 87, 96, 100, 111, 118, 128, 131, 141; chain, 56, 65, 74, 93, 98; Chinese knot, 165; colcha, 15; coral, 59; Cretan, 9, 32, 167; cross-stitch, 12, 56, 83; double knot (Palestrina knot), 93, 96, 100, 122, 128, 129, 170; edging stitches, 86; featherstitch, 74; flame, see BARGELLO; French knot, 18, 33, 41, 69, 103, 112, 141; herringbone, 56, 68; Italian insertion, 88; Palestrina knot, see double knot above; running stitch, 14, 20, 26, 76, 135; satin, 20, 78, 79; sorbello, 164, 169; spiderweb, 59; stem, 26, 93, 125, 149; tent, 20, 21, 83, also see CANVASWORK; Turkeywork, 19, 42, 94, 165; up-and-down buttonhole, 93, 94, 118; Vandyke, 164, 166; whip-stitch, 33, 83, 111. Also see DECORATIVE STITCHES, EMBROIDERY

stuffing, inserting PADDING or other filling such as kapok, foam rubber, or shredded nylon stockings between two layers of fabric to create three-dimensional effects or forms such as PILLOWS. Usually the front and back layer are placed with right sides together, seamed all around except for a small opening for stuffing, turned, and then stuffed. Non-raveling FABRIC such as felt can be sewed on the right side without having to turn it. If stitchery is to be done on a stuffed form, it is usually worked on each piece separately before the piece is assembled and stuffed, 32, 141, also see SOFT SCULPTURE

surface stitchery, see EMBROIDERY

tassels, ornamental tufts of equal length, loose threads. The tassel tops may be made by inserting and COVERING CORKS, 24, 68, 111, 118, 120, 127, 128, 131, also see FRINGING

textile, or fiber, sculpture, see SOFT SCULPTURE

tie-dyeing and tie-bleaching, related FABRIC TECHNIQUES in which cloth is bunched and tied with string or knotted to form resist areas. The uneven penetration of dye or bleach into the fabric forms different patterns according to the pattern of the tying, 125, 148

tracing, see TRANSFERRING DESIGNS

embellished w/ stitchery
appliqué

Star of David   p. 101, 103

To emphasize the shape, the
Central hexagon could have
a solid filling made of massed
Chinese knots. p. 96 or closely
worked satin st. p. 24 in a
contrasting color or weight of thread

Coral Stitch

Hold the thread loosely on the
surface of the fabric w/ your left
thumb (if you are right-handed) to
pull the thread thru the fabric
and over the thread to form a knot, etc.

p. 9

Basic Stitches — page 12, 13, 14.
Th C St Ency.

1. Couching *
2. Herringbone St *
3. Chevron St. *
4. Holbein St. *
5. Split St.
6. Coral St * Special
7. Stem St. favorite
8. Chain St. *
9. Outline St. *
10. Running St. *
11. Feather St. *
12. Blanket St. *
13. Cretan St. * — pretty for leaves
14. Buttonhole st. * — Interlaced buttonhole St. * p. 47
15. Cross st.
16. Darning st *
17. Backstitch *